MIXED EMOTIONS

Edited by

Bobby Tobolik

First published in Great Britain in 2005 by
POETRY NOW
Remus House,
Coltsfoot Drive,
Peterborough, PE2 9JX
Telephone (01733) 898101
Fax (01733) 313524

Copyright Contributors 2005

SB ISBN 1 84602 005 0

FOREWORD

Although we are a nation of poets we are accused of not reading poetry, or buying poetry books. After many years of listening to the incessant gripes of poetry publishers, I can only assume that the books they publish, in general, are books that most people do not want to read.

Poetry should not be obscure, introverted, and as cryptic as a crossword puzzle: it is the poet's duty to reach out and embrace the world.

The world owes the poet nothing and we should not be expected to dig and delve into a rambling discourse searching for some inner meaning.

The reason we write poetry (and almost all of us do) is because we want to communicate: an ideal; an idea; or a specific feeling. Poetry is as essential in communication, as a letter; a radio; a telephone, and the main criterion for selecting the poems in this anthology is very simple: they communicate.

CONTENTS

DAYDREAMER'S DELIGHT

I write to incite, to inspire my mind
Thought-provoking, philosophical investigating
Brain impulses elevated through the pen
Over and over, again and again

I like to dream, I like to write
A passion with unbounded site.
Nothing is too vast
It's all in my clasp
Creative writing, I find it enticing

Where do the thoughts come from?
The heart, soul or the mind
Or perhaps a combination of the three
Makes me, makes we, think the way we be!

Whatever the cause, I know the effect
Daydreamer I do profess
Writer I do, and aspire to be
I know it is, what makes me, me.

Sheridan Buckley

BURST

And I feel my heart close
Never to trust again
And she's smiling now
She doesn't know
The sweet pain that drips from your pen

Seducing and manipulating words
That turn and burst
Allegiance and integrity completely cursed . . .

Viv Westbrook

GUILTY

The feeling of guilt I must say
Is just something that gets in our way
To deal with the fact and try to extract
From a torment that won't go away

Our own sense of being is a threat
If self honour just cannot be met
Though to fall into the trap
Would be a mishap, so be the person you are for today

You know why you feel guilty and so
These thoughts of it you must now throw
Get back on track, decide the right pack
Now forget today and live for tomorrow

S C Matthews

LOVE IS LIFE

Love is life, life is love,
Hold me tight tonight my love.
As I lay here in the surroundings of love
I thank the Lord from Heaven above
For being surrounded in so much love.
As I awake feeling fresh as a rose
Knowing I am loved wherever I go
My eyes sparkle, my hair glows,
I feel lovely wherever I go.
This magical thing called love is so special
It warms you through and through,
It also radiates you through
Like the rainbow of life.

Denise McDonald

HER DAY

She wakes at first light of dawn,
Bedroom curtains swiftly drawn.
Sunlight floods the room a-blazing,
In its warmth, her body bathing.

Pads slowly to the 'little room'
Nature calls! Her body she grooms.
Ablutions done, she treads the stairs,
Of her nakedness, she never cares.

She attends her morning needs
Breakfast of toast and sesame seeds.
Still naked, in all her glory,
She's alone, no one to tell her story.

Her clothes, simple yet smart,
Each morning she dresses the part.
Cotton blouse, cool and crisp,
Long skirt, of chiffon wisp.

Flat shoes for added comfort,
No cause to take a second look.
To vanish in the crowd,
Yet, of her body she is proud.

Day done she returns to 'home'
Her little haven, her very own.
Divesting of her outer shell,
Once again, she is the one, she knows so well . . .

Alan J Morgan

WITHIN THE WALLS OF DARKNESS

The walls close in; as if death himself,
Has sent along his morbid calling card
Blackness comes as fantasies of weird things
Which invade my already disturbed mind
Seeing fairies, ghosts and werewolves
In a place where the sane are made insane
In a place where you live within yourself
Locked up; strapped up; left alone
A place called an asylum; a loony bin;
A mental hospital, for the disturbed
Call it what you may; it is all one
Where reality is made unreal
Where the spirits and shadows
Play upon the long, wide, white, blank walls
A sudden jolt, a sudden push
No one to see, no one to care
Just the four bare walls to surround you
Just four walls that are around you
Whilst you calmly walk
Round and round and round
People look, laugh and point
Look there's that lunatic!
Look there's that psychopath
What do they know?
What strange things move and go bump
In the blackness of the night
Why alien beings awake and talk
To me at night; they prod and inject liquids
Something cold is then released
Within my very soul
Then I imagine I am invisible;

I imagine I am so powerful
It goes on and on
But when the real darkness appears
A nurse in her white and blue uniform comes
She smiles; she injects and goes away
I am then bought into the world of reality
Until tomorrow that is!

Maria Sheikh

THE MIRROR

As I watched the mirror washing and rolling down
In a cacophony of sound
I looked into the mirror and saw my reflection
I asked myself
'Who am I?'
My reflection didn't reply
An undecided girl looked back
Who was this girl?
Was she new?
Was she old?
Was she me staring back?
Was she who I wanted to be?
Was she who everyone wanted me to be?
Was she who I was turning into?
These questions popped into my mind
This girl wasn't my kind
I didn't want to be noticed
But I didn't want to go invisible
She just winked at me
As if I knew the answer
Still I cannot decide as
I look today in that crystal pool of tears I cried.

Darrion Warwick-Hart

REST IN PEACE MY CHILD
(For Becky and Emily)

Lay your head upon your pillow
Your problems they will keep
Until another sunrise
But for the moment, sleep
For the dawning will bring
Another war to fight
So while you are sleeping
Let your fantasies take flight

Let angels come to guard you
While you are having rest
For tomorrow will bring with it
More problems to test
So let your strength build within you
For another war-torn day
And I am here to help you
If you turn to me and pray.

Grace Divine

BEAUTIFUL BABY GIRL

A beautiful baby girl I see
sitting peacefully upon your knee
such lovely eyes and glowing cheeks
it's nice to know she's yours for keeps
you'll always be there at her side
to love and help and be her guide
all the memories are there to share
and for you to show you really care
so when you put her down to sleep
give her a kiss upon the cheeks
and when she wakes up in the night
make sure you're there to hold her tight

Helen Church

UNKNOWN ZONE

When I'm alone in the unknown zone
There's only abstract relations and false sensations
Floating adrift after the rift, feeling forlorn after the storm
Isolated and frustrated - diffusion and confusion
Having been projected and then rejected
Totally disenchanted because my wishes were never granted
Abolished and demolished
Cos contradiction only creates friction
A perception with no connection
With the divide on one side - fracture and rapture
Seriously mystic yet antagonistic
So should I bond or abscond? Link or sink?
Germinate or terminate
Are we finished or undiminished
Void or eternally undestroyed
Cos the workings of my mind can sometimes be cruel and unkind
So instead I'll work creatively with my hands in the sand
Until you eventually understand
That at least I tried to be faithful and unified
I refrained and sustained again and again
Cos I can never be used, so I remain unbruised
Outspoken and unbroken
Against the battle of wills and all other ills
The tug of love in Heaven above
So don't rearrange, please just try to change
Because I can untwist everything with my wrist
And my imminent landing will remove all misunderstanding
When taking a vacation to my original destination
And so my love I'll send to where the rainbow ends
Where I'll find purity and finally reach maturity.

Tina Snowdon

MASTERPIECES
(08.30)

No more masterpieces
Flow from his pen
Since the disintegration
Of them; crumbling conversations
And burst brows; *over*, tightrope
Walking for fun, for devilment:
Over, the holding on;
Clever wordplay
And travelling miles to
One another . . .
Oh, welcome to the
Art of losing; diplomas
Hang on his and hers
Shaded wall; shadows
Cast on lungs, boarded
Floors and lives;
Over, the vitriolic lyrics
And nastiness and
Beauty; *over*, all,
But the final fling
And his final masterpiece . . .
The precise packing
Of his bag; the precise breaking of her
Heart . . .

Bill Talbott

2004

A new year begins, another one ends
Celebrating with family and friends
Another year, new resolutions
Building bridges, finding solutions

Prince Harry in trouble, silly lad
Smoking and drinking, it's just a fad
He's a royal, a rebel; he'll soon be a man
He'll wed one day to a royal fan

Talking of royals, disgraces and such
Beckham in trouble, should look and not touch
His wife so forgiving, soft in the head
Saw text messages that weren't to be read

The war in Iraq, it was a disgrace
They treated so badly the human race
Let there be peace and goodwill to all men
Maybe one day, don't know when

The year ended badly with the tsunami wave
We rallied round, our help we gave
Many buildings destroyed and lives were lost
Can never be replaced at any cost

A new year begins, another one ends
Celebrating with family and friends
Another year, new resolutions
Building bridges, finding solutions.

Jacqui Wicks

CAFE SOCIETY

Images iconic continental
adorn our famous street

The trend to sup alfresco
on boulevards wide that claim.
The Paris, who spawned the culture
our cafe society meet.

The people watching syndrome
a Champs Elyses' tale.

Observing the human traffic
content to sit and stare,
imbibing the latest coffee
our palate follows the trail.

From the rich and dark espresso
cappuccino's creamy crust.

Amidst a sea of people
we spill and overflow.
To the pale opalescent latte
a langue-de-chat a must.

From 'Hemingway' and the Rue Bonaparte
to Sartre and the Cafe de Flore.

To the Rue de Seine and Cafe Palette
and Saint-Germain-Des-Pres.
We raise our cups on Lord Street
our Le Precope of today.

Edna M Sarsfield

POETS' DREAMS

To perceive a thought, write it down
Wrapped in velvet, worn as a crown
From the heart, loving the thought
From the mind, where words are taught
From the eye, we have seen
From these, poetic words we glean

The golden light of dawn, the grass of green
Silver droplets of rain that gleam
Fit for the fairy queen, for magic
In this prism is seen spells of wonder
In the rainbow as the promise we redeem
Or so it may seem, just another dream

The fleetness of the gazelle
Or the fairies in their dell
Words of fantasy, we love so well
Or visit our own private hell
On all this the poet will dwell
Of love and the witches' spell

The poets' heaven or hell
Words of healing, words of hurt
Words of peace, words of war
Words from the past or days to come
Travelling through time, from shore to shore
Poets' words for evermore

Anne Marshall

MY POEM

I dreamt of you
among thousands of raindrops
on the pane of a bus
sat on the last row
of a dark, suburban cinema
amongst the notes of an old track
which the radio plays
among the hive
which advance targetless

I dreamt of you
because it was right
because I felt it was stronger than me

Maybe you can feel
my veins at this moment
my pulse in a cardiac dance
in a sea flow
like a cellular storm

or maybe you can forget me.

Ivan Berta

THE PICNIC

The picnic was fine till the ants joined in,
The little wretches can't half bite,
We threw the rest in the bin,
Then went off to fly the kite,
That got tangled up in the tree,
Lesley climbed up to set it free,
After that, we went home for tea.

P Wright

OH LOVE!

I wonder how you are fashioned
For you are from the Almighty
That's why you are appreciated
Appreciated by all who
Know your worth and ability

Through you one saw one
Eagerly one proposed to one
With deep fear in the heart
Fear of the outcome
Also fear of what the future holds
Besides, they agree in union

And soon the fear disappears
Brought about by a confidence
These hearts are in union
The union was made by nature
And in space of time you germinate seed
And bear fruit, love.

Ogbodo John Obinna

MEMORIES

Flickering faces on an old reel
To grandchildren holds no appeal
Beautiful girls in black and white
In films shown early in the night

Now in the flesh seem plain and aged
Old ladies by youth's ways enraged
Wear crisp white perms and flowered frocks
Tell stories while we watch the clocks

Charlie Middlemass

ONE FILLED WITH JOY PREACHES WITHOUT PREACHING

I have studied under many teachers for ten years
but I've learnt nothing from them for they had only tears.
I wanted to know the joy of being alive
and they offered me a pool of depression to dive.

Somehow one day, I came across this child.
He was running round and round being wild.
He knew he was running for no reason yet, he was filled with joy.
He had no candy to please him, yet, high-spirited was that boy!

He ran and pulled his sister's hair.
He got scolded by his mom but he didn't care.
He ran again, stumbled over a rock and fell.
He then stood up quickly and left smiling without a yell.

He looked plain and he looked poor.
Still, he was happy and contented to the core.
There were so few toys for him to play.
Still, he enjoyed those and did not flay.

This very little child immediately touched my heart.
There are many to aim at the bull's eye but success came
only to his dart,
for others spoke of joy and weren't joyful in living.
As for this boy, he was joyful and this is how, he has preached
without preaching.

Sichu Mali

COLTRANA BARNABY BEAR

Before Barney we had two black labs, which did what they were told
At 14 years they passed away because they were quite old
My husband had a brainwave after a year or two
Said we should have another dog, a Newfoundland breed will do
We visited Pat and Karen who said most of the litter were sold
Pat told us she had only one pup left even though they were 3 weeks old
We named our puppy Barney, and waited while he grew
We couldn't wait to take him home; when we did the days just flew
7 months have passed and Barney developed a mind of his own
He now decides if he'll go for a walk or just remain at home
He plays a game with my husband; I think that it's called *Dare*
With one foot on the settee 'you can tell he wants to sit there'
The labs we had did not push it, but with Barney it's a wonderful game
To try and make us give in, I'm sure is Barney's aim
His favourite spot is the fireplace; it's made of marble you know
We cannot have the fire on because he refuses to go
He loves to walk into Scarborough, everyone thinks he's great
He gives his paw and slobbers them; their hands get in a state
It takes an hour to walk 10 yards with everyone stroking his head
I get asked many questions like, 'Does he sleep in your bed?'
I tell them of the stair gate that is firmly fixed to the wall
At the moment he cannot open it, but he's growing and getting quite tall
His paws are large and hold much mud, the carpet is past repair
But we wouldn't be without him, our wonderful Barnaby Bear.

Sue Brooks

CHANGING ROOM - THE BLUE LAGOON

At once beautiful and obscene,
The naked bodies of old women
Insult my senses. Hanging flesh
And scar marks, all subtleties and
Figurations left somewhere. Somewhere lost.

The nubile young avoid staring,
Avoid truth and belief,
And change in private.
And in-between, somewhere
Beyond lost youth but decades
From the ravages of age
I wander, immodest, bare,
Celebrating my flesh
Which, given circumstance,
Is alive and whole
And for just one moment,
Almost divine.

Val Wild

LOVE

Love has many meanings
Amongst us human beings,
A baby's smile so tender and true,
The love one has for the sky so blue.
The love for God,
Who gave us flowers,
The birds and trees,
To pass happy hours.

A Bishop

OCCULTATION

I glanced up at the evening sky,
Luminous
With fading blue light.

The thinnest sliver of new moon
And a perfect diamond
Sparkling at one curved horn.

'A satellite,' said my mother,
As we followed the diamond,
Moving through the darkening sky.

Planet of love, the newspapers told us
The next morning,
An occultation of Venus.

I felt privileged,
At the wonderfully unexpected gift,
A glimpse into another universe.

Veena Chalam

LIGHT AT MY WINDOW
(For Mum)

Light at my window
Gentle, seeking
Beyond, there is joy,
'Joy shall come in the morning'
Now, you dance again,
Are young again
In morning vast, full
Of gull call, voice
Of sea, path of tremulous
Illumination where we know
Love shall never die.

George Coombs

WHEN SHADOWS FALL

(Written through the eyes of an Alzheimer's sufferer)

I find myself on a strange adventure
A lone traveller,
On a journey wrapped in a cloak of mystery
To a destiny unknown.
Scenes flash by as I travel on.
Places I've known, people I've met,
Strange encounters - remote
Beyond recall.

As I journey on, lie unmapped landscapes.
Tunnels of mist close round me.
Ghostly figures, unfamiliar voices beckon me
To where? I do not know.
For I am lost.

Sometimes shafts of light pierce the darkness,
When shutters of understanding unfold
Like butterflies' wings in flight.
For I see a well known face.
A hand reaches out and grasps mine,
I hold on so tightly, all fear has gone.
The mists lift, if, but for a moment.
No longer a lone traveller
For my loved one is here with me.

On and on I travel,
Day by day, year by year
In a world of my own.
Encircling arms of love always enfold me
Like a warm blanket on a snowy day.
The journey is called *the long goodbye*
The long farewell to journey's end.

Frances M Gorton

SHADOW DANCER

Long dark shadows run from her toes
A dancer in silhouette creates her prose
With a few soft silken movements she begins to talk
Her stillness is silence and she begins to walk
Long strides denote words seldom heard before
A long and slender shadow follows behind on the floor

Cascading hair gleams and falls with grace
Swirling and curling covering her face
She carries on her poetry and she moves again
But stumbles and glides to where her shadow had lain
Her words stop flowing and the dark shapes are no more
A hand brushes her forehead, it is the shadow from the floor

It surrounds her broken spirit with a plethora of new words
They rise together singing, arms fluttering like birds
They speak in angelic chorus with notes high and long
Turning their words into sonnets and sonnets into song
A paleness now dampens their bright moon's glow
They silently watch shadows fade and slowly go

The sun casts a new theme a rich golden haze
Mist becomes their music and they dance in a daze
Talking in gestures rhyming rhythmically and grand
The dew takes the place of shadows where they stand
Silencing their dance and with a garland in her hair
She pirouettes under crown in a radiance filled air

Their words have been spoken in a dance now complete
A cool wind rolls wrapping leaves around still feet
She looks up from the earth and the shadow isn't there
As she tilts her head to the warm sun's harsh glare
Her gaze is stolen by the woods and chinks of light at play
On the shadow dancer interwoven in the trees as they sway.

Anita Maina Kulkarni

AUTUMN

Someone has lit a bonfire,
Someone is burning leaves,
The glow is orange and ruby,
Smoke goes up through the trees.

Boys throw stones at branches
For conkers hidden from view,
They fall from prickly cases,
Polished and shiny new.

Mists in the early morning,
A sharp blue sky at noon,
Violet clouds at sunset
Before the harvest moon.

Hedges are rich with berries,
Scarlet and inky-blue,
Orchards are heavy with apples,
Pears are ripening too.

This is the season of gaining
The profits of sun and rain
Till the earth returns to stillness,
Waiting for spring again.

Neil Adams

GET WELL DAD

I hope you get better soon,
So I can take you to the moon.
And when we get back,
We can have a snack.
From the *bottom* of my heart,
Love Kyle.

Kyle Rowe

Harbour Wall

The man stands at the harbour wall
He's taking in the view
The man stands at the harbour wall
He's feeling rather blue
And he's wondering what his life was like
All those years ago
And he's wondering where his children went
Now they're so far away
And he doesn't get a single call
Their lives must be OK
And day by day he wonders
About things he's said and done
And wouldn't it be wonderful
If he could see his sons
He's standing at the harbour wall
The sun comes shining through
And he's writing on his postcard now
It would be nice
To be with you
The man walks down the leafy path
He's noticing the time
The man sees shadows on the ground
Then the sun is going down
And he's planning his tomorrows
With his family in mind
The man stands at the crossroads
In his body and his mind
And he's shrugging off mistakes he's made
And resolves to make them good
And he's thinking of good times they had
And when they might call him Dad?

Gillian Brown

BEAUTY LIES IN THE EYES

Beauty lies in the eyes of the beholder,
An open flower,
A flying bird,
A sunset sky,
A baby playing with rings,
A kindly deed whate'er your race,
A fruit that's ripe,
A laughing open face.

Beauty lies in the eyes of the beholder,
A windswept grass,
A sturdy tree,
A still sea calm,
A thoughtful glance with aid,
A playful puppy jumping high,
A throwing ball,
A laughing catch well made.

Beauty lies in the eyes of the beholder,
A boat-tossed sea,
A lightning flash,
An action man,
A woman swimming free,
A water skier still upright,
A football goal,
A distant glorious sight.

Ben Henderson Smith

SHIPMAN

The face stares out from a thousand pictures,
Hirsute, respectable, bespectacled.
But the eyes . . .
Is there an eternal soul behind their blank and clueless stare
Or do they simply reflect the illness of our times?
He came to many in hypocratic agency.
Some may have dreaded death,
Few would have chosen death,
But none was offered clemency.

His voice would soothe and reassure
While his hand applied
The false, sharp Nemesis.
But the eyes . . .
Were they smiling, softly comforting
At the end? As he ushered them
To kingdom come, did the cool light of reason
Flare into the glare of crazed insanity?

What should we do with him?
Can we, or they that mourn ever forgive him?
Should we share blame for whatever outrages
In his life have turned his mind to callous slaughter?
We might.
But the eyes . . .
Will still stare out, mocking, unrepentant.

Gerry Robertson

THE MIRROR LIES

The mirror lies.
Her image stands before her now,
with livid marks to cheek and brow,
the hunched, and twisted, awkward frame;
a form that wears her name.
With searching eyes
she looks beyond the carapace
of ugly body, ugly face,
to find the graceful, loving soul;
the person who is whole.
For finally, she knows it now,
and wonders when, and wonders how,
she taught herself to self-despise,
and own the mirror lies.

The mirror lies
are what they fed her, year by year;
eroding with an acid fear
her happiness, to leave a void;
her confidence destroyed.
And no disguise
could hide the burning shame within,
each time they made her face a sin
of imperfection in her mind;
repugnancy defined.
Destroying the innocence of youth
they made her face the ugly truth
that brought her to internalise
the hated mirror lies.

The mirror lies
in shards of triumph on the ground.
Rejoicing the freedom found,
she smashes what has kept her chained
until their power waned.
She's cut the ties.
A piece held in a bloodied fist
is laid against a white-scarred wrist.
She does not cut; she has no cause
but, in that moment's pause,
remembers wishing she had died
with each attempted suicide,
and hears again the unheard cries
against the mirror lies.

The mirror lies!
Reflections from a worldly light
too often blind the inner sight,
but as he sees her, she sees too,
and hope is born anew.
His love is wise.
The beauty of each child who's made
in love's own image, is displayed
nowhere in any outer part,
but only in the heart.
And now there's no disparity;
she sees herself with clarity,
for in a baby's loving eyes
the real mirror lies.

Ruth Walmsley

UNTITLED

A tale I heard from relatives
Down in the smoke
Underneath the flight path of Heathrow
Their cat called Gin
They had lost him
And buried him some while ago.
Opening up the door one morning
Sitting sheltered by the awning
Was a ginger kitten just like Gin
The markings were so familiar
They were the same, not even similar
It was a shock, and straightaway he came in
He ran to the corner under the sink
Without hesitation
Gin's meals were always put down there
Was the scent still on the air?
That must be the explanation
They gave the kitten food to sup
And after he was polished up
He made off with determination
Took the sofa in his stride
And atop the cabinet wide
Sniffed and circled in investigation
Something's missing, he seemed to say
Gin's basket was brought without delay
Now this is comfort this is, eh!

The kit had settled on the spot
The previous pet had spent his lot
It was like he'd never been away
Hairs raised upon necks
The freaked-out humans said, 'By heck!
What about him!'

The little creature shone his eye
And,
Without a lie,
It was Gin.

V Jenkins

THE MISSING LINK

It's invisible you know
This bond,
This link,
This time that flows between
Our bodies
Yet cannot be broken
By others.

I need you . . . often
Even though I am sinking
Down, into a dream world of both
Thought and illusion.

The fear it grips me.
And then I cannot connect
To those who see
A different soul before them.

They don't understand
Or need to. I like the madness
It's mine to own,
Publish and be damned.

Anita Ann McNamee

TOWN TALK

I want
To see
The town tonight
To help to sing the lullaby
That makes the town sleep
To tell a tale
Of towering structures
And the twinkle
Of silvery moonbeams
Synchronised with
Night lights
Of the town
That tweet a tune
About darkness
Ameliorated
Gentle urbanity
Lights that toast
The triumph
Of the town.

C D Smith

I THINK OF YOU

I think of you when the morning light
punctures my tiny room
and I would like to think you might
come to me when the day is brighter,
stay with me until night falls
and warm away the gloom of midnight
when dreams can frighten sense and hope away.

Fred Brown

SHE

She smokes until she can smoke no more,
She drinks until she hits the floor,
She takes them 'til she gets so high,
She cries until it hurts her eyes,
She breathes until she's lost all hope,
And now she just begins to choke.

She watched until her world caved in,
She hid until she found her sin,
She fell until there seemed no end,
She stayed until her heart could not mend,
She listened until her ears were deaf,
Now what has she got left?

She was real until she faded away,
She was here until that day,
She was me until I was her,
Did that silence need to stir?

Gemma Mackay

QUESTIONS

Would there be love without hate?
Is there a chance for us to control our own fate?
What about pleasure if there never was any pain?
Could you ever lose if nothing was to gain?
How about joy if we never felt sorrow?
Should one live just for today, forget about tomorrow?
Who can you trust if they only feed us lies?
Where will I find the answers to every single why?

Olli Suntinen

BUTTONS

In this age in which we live,
No need to work or think.
Just press the right button,
Your problems just solved in a blink.

If you are in need of money,
A button you can press,
But money isn't honey,
If deeply in debt.

If the right button you cannot press,
This problem you can soon address,
Just press the right buttons,
To tell you the right button to press.

With all the buttons we do press,
The most important ones forget,
Soon in the hands of the village cop,
When your own trousers they do drop.

Press that certain button,
Contact the one you adore.
Press the one next to it
And you could start a war.

When computers press their own buttons
And give us all the sack,
For the want of a funny story,
They will soon ask for us back.

Now how will folks make love?
How will they get satisfactions?
They will simply press a button,
I leave the rest to your imagination.

But how will babies be made?
Fast and efficient no doubt,
Just press the belly button,
Then the designer baby drops out.

For the last line of this poem,
I have not got a clue,
There isn't a button to press
So I will leave it to one of you.

W H Stevens

MY UNCLE GEORGE

Many, many years ago,
a mother cried with joy,
as here among the humble folk
she gave birth to her first boy.

His days of childhood quickly passed,
school days were left behind,
he joined the forces - went to war -
and was sent to the front line.

He came back minus his right arm,
but his spirit did not bend,
he faced his life with courage,
and would until the end.

Now here among the humble folk,
his life draws to its end.
My dear beloved uncle George,
a gentleman - a friend.

Alma Sutton

THE LOGIC OF LOVE

Love - isn't every lover sometimes a poet?

Some people can write a song or a poem describing the emotions that love can arouse, passions, desires, sometimes the pain - yet for others their feelings are hard to explain!

What does it mean - that look between you? There are crowds all around, but all you can see is that one special face. The night may be dark, a frost in the air, but for lovers the night seems a wonderful place!

How can it be that a voice can thrill, send a chill, or a touch of the hand becomes a caress? Who can define that yearning inside - those long, lonely hours, when the one you that you love is far from your side?

Is a mortal lost in a world so unreal, that the sound of birdsong and the falling rain, suddenly becomes a stirring refrain?

The moon and stars are simply part of the galaxy, light years away, yet a dreamer makes them into a wonderful fantasy. A bright ray of light - bringing the lovelorn a message of hope - is a moonbeam really such a mystical sight?

Now a touch of the lips, is that not a natural way of expression, so why does it cause such amazing reaction? A heart beating fast, a sigh from the soul, a whole new world is beginning to form, all this just from one kiss?

Rational, indeed, for the young to seek love, the reasoning clear, so why doesn't time clearly define that love is only for those in their prime?

Ageless, it seems, is that driving force, from dewy-eyed youth to the mellowing years.

And the words, so simple they are - I love you! How can three little words rule the world - all the songs and music, cards and bouquets, the novels and films, with only one theme - I love you?

Do you see what I mean? Isn't every lover sometimes a poet? Doesn't every person have a dream? Yet, when the logic of love is made apparent - who will care when caught in love's spell?

Ros Heller

THE DUCKLING

He was a feckless duckling, so cheeky and so proud,
Who thought his mum and family a mincing maudlin crowd.
He thought himself so grown-up, he didn't need advice,
He'd do just what he wanted to, which wasn't very nice.

'O children, please be careful, and play within the reed,'
His frantic mother pleaded, her siblings taking heed -
Except this feckless duckling, his nose up in the air,
Who put his oary feet right down, and paddled out of there.

He sailed into the middle with quack, quack, quack, quack, quack,
Head held high up to the sky, and then came sailing back.
He looked into the water, o what a handsome face -
And that was that, the mirror spat, he'd gone without a trace.

His mother looked about her, she'd seen it all before,
There was the faintest ripple with a feather floating o'er.
She gathered all her nestlings and told them what to do,
Yet one by one, as always, her duckling's feathers flew.

Derek Haskett-Jones

YOUR EARTH ANGEL

I'm out of this world
A heavenly girl
Your Earth angel
Here to make you all happy and well,
Everywhere I go
It's love I show.
I'm working for God
That's my job,
To make this world a happy place
Put a smile on everyone's face.
I'm a sunshine girl
Your Earth angel,
With my beautiful smile
I'll make your lives worthwhile,
Brightening everyone's day
As I go on my way.
For all of you I do care
Giving out love everywhere,
There's no clouds in the sky
When I pass by,
All you will find
Is lots of sunshine,
I'm loving and giving, caring and kind
Giving out love, *love* divine,
Lots of smiles, kisses and hugs,
Says all of you, 'I do love.'
One look at me, you it will tell
With my golden hair and curls
That I'm a very loving girl
Here on Earth as your angel . . .

Lindy Roberts

FINANCIAL MESS

Financial stress, financial mess,
Debt depression, debt distress.

What I see I want, what I want I get.
Overdrafts, loans, store cards and Visa,
Getting it on credit couldn't be any easier.

Shopping is a buzz, yeah a real big thrill,
The problems only start when I receive the bill.

Robbing Peter to pay Paul,
Never earning enough to cover them all.

I carry on regardless; bury my head in the sand,
Never having a penny left in the palm of my hand.

Now it's a problem, but no one understands,
I don't owe out hundreds, I owe out grands!

It's no longer any fun; I don't sleep at night,
When I do I wake up screaming with terrible fright.

How can I buy food or put petrol in the car,
Swept away by a tide of debt and the shore seems so far.

I borrow more; it's a temporary fix,
Loans I'll be repaying till I'm 106.

I could lose my house; I could lose my car,
How could I have let things get this far?

I can't see a way out and start to despair,
Who can I turn to, would anybody care?

They're gonna send the bailiffs who'll take away my stuff,
I used to live in luxury, but pretty soon I'll be living rough.

It's all my own fault, yeah that much is true,
This is happening to me but how easily could it be you?

Robbie Shorey

FUNERAL OF EFFORTS

After all I've put in
This is how you repay me

You take me aside
Tell me I've been replaced
By someone older, apparently wiser than me
Who you've met on a single occasion

Heads will roll;
I was the last to know
My own fate
'Friends' dropping camouflaged hints
Blinded by foolishness took them as mere jokes

Standing outside you
Reconsidering the inside
Judge and jury
Bribed by demon perched upon shoulder
White winged figure lay motionless at its bias feet

Pressure building
I plate myself with an imaginary humour of it all
Inside I am ablaze; my friends
Now enemies
My hands be stilled

In my mind they are clasped
Around your neck
Squeezing the ungrateful soul from the heartless tomb
In which it resides with such cowardice
Thoughts could never come to pass

My tongue hushed by white winged figure
Demon caged,
But slowly picking the lock
It yearns to be free to roar
To signal my soul's call of distress
To announce my disgust
To unleash its wrath
To sound the unanswered question

Why?

Simon Audis

THE PROMISE

You promised you'd never leave me,
each day you said as much.
Said we'd spend our lives together
you're here, but can't feel my touch.

You promised you'd never leave me
said we'd never be apart.
Where are you now that I need you?
I'm alone with a breaking heart.

You promised you'd never leave me,
I still talk to you endlessly.
Sometimes I feel that you hear me
from the shadows, I think you see.

I promise I'll never leave you.
There's a light in your eyes at will.
You hold my hand so tightly,
through Alzheimer's you remember me still.

Valerie Wyatt

THE GREATEST SIN

Three sins, which grieve the heart of Christ,
For the serpent works both day and night.
Abortion is the greatest sin,
Satanic words an evil spin.

A failed excuse to justify,
Poor little souls to limbo fly.
The sadists with satanic rites,
Innocent children they sacrifice.

The paedophile, a child he's stalking,
Immoral abuse a dead man walking.
Humanist mothers with selfish hearts,
Murderous surgery ripping babies apart.

GfB

MY FAMILY

My family is a strange one; I will be the first one to admit.
We are a unit of mix and match, of allsorts . . . and a bit!
Now take my daughter of thirteen years, I wish someone would,
I will never understand her ways; I'll just knock my head on wood!
My eldest boy has found his way, after long and rocky path
He just pops back, for home-cooked meals, and a nice hot bubble bath!
My youngest boy is full of fun, laughter, tears and enthusiasm
But tests my patience, and often wishes someone else would have him!
My middle boy makes sense to me, although I'm told he's autistic
I know where I am with him, because he is so honest and ritualistic!
A mother's love is unconditional, in my weekly magazine I once read
My middle son just smiled and said, 'You'll get a rest Mum, when
you're dead!'

Alison Mitchell

THE SASSUNACHS

Auld Scotland was invaded in nineteen seventy-one,
The sassunachs cam' drivin' up an' fairly made us run,
They emptied oot the larder an' sent us oot for pies,
An' ate the hale clamjamphrie before oor very eyes.

They sprawled a' ower the settee, dropped litter on the rug,
Left a'thing scattered ower the hoose, an' feared the very dug,
They played the telly morn an' nicht an' spun the records roon,
Run hot water in the bath oh! whit a quine an' loon.

His mither phoned her wonder boy to see if he was fine,
Sleeping weel an' eatin' weel, she was up to ninety-nine,
Kathleen's fairy roon the twist, demented, high an' queer,
An' soon had Nana an' Granda in a proper state o' fear.

They lorded it for ae' hale week, an' treated us like slaves,
If they'd stayed another day we'd sure be in oor graves,
He guzzled cakes an' meat an' pies, drank orange an' Ribena,
But the finest sight in a' the land was 'the back of their Cortina'.

Tammy D

ALWAYS RUNNING

I can't keep crying, I'm running out of tears
I can't keep screaming, I'm running out of words
I can't keep denying, I'm running out of excuses
I can't keep lying, I'm running out of stories
I can't keep fighting, I'm running out of strength
I can't keep hiding, I'm running out of time
I can't keep up the act, I'm running out of illusions
I can't keep up with life, I'm running out of faith
I can't keep up the running, I'm running out of distance.

Mark A Games

WRONG AGAIN

You don't do it like that
That's what they say
You're doing it wrong
That's not the way

Whatever we do
It's bound to be wrong
We've heard it before
It's the same old song

It's never just right
I told you so
Do it like me
I'm a know-all you know

Do your own thing
That's what I say
You may get it wrong
But you'll learn more that way

John Ridgway

GHOST

Where am I?
Why was I here?
Why were the days so bright and misty?
I wander to and fro
Searching for the answer to my prayer,
Drifting, floating, no one to see me
Passing through the day.
I breathe between lines of memory,
I perish each moment
I walk this Earth.

R Sunshine

TSUNAMI

The tsunami broke taking thousands of lives
Husbands, daughters, sons and wives
Mothers, fathers, no one was spared
As nature roared and her venom she bared
In towns and villages on the beach in the sun
Her raging vengeance could not be outrun
The devastation, despair and lost souls
The tears and terror as it all unfolds
As the whole world over is mournful and sad
Doing all that they can, for this thing so bad
Mere human beings with hearts full of sorrow
Doing all that's good, no thoughts of tomorrow
These deeds need doing, need doing today
They give gifts, presents, and some of their pay
We must do this for hope and belief
To show the world, we share in their grief.

Paul Sullivan

IDLE DREAMS

A dream, the memory of a loved one
    What treasures play in the mind
Fleeting moments of regret and joy
    Tragically left behind.

Do you remember that smile?
    Do you remember the tears?
Do you remember the worries?
    Do you remember the fears?

Oh, to see that smile again
    To hear the laughter of joy
I'd do all the things I never did
    And proudly say, 'That's my boy.'

John Morrison

SAFE AS HOUSES

Am I mad
Or just eccentric?
The medical term is agoraphobic.

As I feel the world outside, is full of fright
That disturbs my sleep all through the night
Until I dream, how amazing
All those different streets, that I am exploring
With no fear, no heavy heart
I can't wait for my dream time to start
For my adventures to begin at last
Why does the night-time go so fast?

When or where will I go?
Will it rain, hail or even snow?
It doesn't matter as I step outside the door
As I am not frightened any more.

I feel safe as houses in my sleep
It's the world outside that makes me frail.

Darren Babbage

LOVE'S STING

Behold the beauty of a rose
dewy droplets glistening
like jewels upon its petals,
feel how velvety soft it is to touch
born upon thorny stems
that doth sting if plucked
yet see how elegant
one rose in a vase doth look.

Lilian Pickford-Miller

A Mother's Love

My beautiful, freckled, fair-faced lad
What a blessing I have had
Your eyes so deep, your heart so wide
Oh, what can I say
About this handsome lad of mine?

With so much love
Instilled in you
A proud mother; I am so true
Your happiness encases me
With love to hold till eternity.

A bonding that will always grow
Never falter, as we both know
Our rubbing noses; our many laughs
A treasure that you cannot surpass.

A gift given from up above
To give your brother and sisters
So much love
You will always be a part of me
A ring of love, eternally.

L Wall

Lonely

Welcome to the land of the broken-hearted,
Friendship and joy have long departed,
Darkness and sorrow now my only friend,
As I patiently wait for this life to end.

Christopher Belton

ON THAT CHRISTMAS DAY

So dewy, was that glorious morning of Christmas
As I was woken by the knock of Santa Claus,
I looked up the blue sky and knew at once
The day was going to be frolicsome, no flaws.

Upwards and downwards were people on the street,
I gazed astonishingly as it held my breath,
Why the litter everywhere with beverage and meat,
Then I remembered it was the Christmas heat.

While exploring the subtopias of the city
In my swallow tailed coat and on my head, a derby
I encountered a party and I was so happy
To have such fun on a Christmas Saturday.

In that Xmas mood frozen
I thought, I was in a terrestrial heaven
But when all was broken and the day darkened
I knew, it was only a festive season.

Raymond A Uyok

AUTUMN

A mber lights in the foliage glowing
U mber, russet, red, under pale blue skies.
T he rose petals fading, the colours going,
U gliness intrudes as the sweet flower dies.
M any a distant evening star lonely gleams
N umberless, uncounted, like our hopeless dreams.

C M Welch

SHINE INSIDE

Whenever I look at the sky
I wonder why

Why should I
Climb all mountains high?

I know sky is impossible to reach

Why should I believe
Having money is being rich

If there's nothing underneath?

And why

I wonder if there is an explanation
All people of this nation
Running against their thoughts

Nobody will find happiness
If not getting nothing less
What's asking for their hearts!

Tatiana Bonatti Peres

YOUR HEART IS MINE

I will go down on my knees,
As you stand before me tall,
I will let your power engulf me,
I know I'll never fall.

The pain inside still burns you,
The wounds are etched so deep,
Let me give you back a soul,
Your heart is mine to keep.

Carolyn Atkinson

A GOOD DEED IS A GOOD SEED

(In memory of a beggar)

I remember you don't I?
You were the one who gave me the 50p,
when I was begging in the tube last summer
when everyone else looked at me like I was scum
when I sat on the floor, in the middle of the tube
trying to play, '*God save the Queen*', on that traffic cone

Made you all laugh though didn't I?

Well at least I did that

Well to me
it did more than that
it made me look at myself and that
and realised just how lucky I am
to be sitting where I am
instead of where you were

Well do you know what I did with the 50p
No! I didn't buy drink
or a 'smoke' with it
I bought some crisps and shared it with the others

So that day you helped much more than me

You helped them too.

Collin Hinds

HEADING ON

As I was walking down the street,
I met a friend of mine,
Problem was, he'd passed away,
Some years before his time!
I said I thought that he was dead,
He said, 'My boy it's true,
But should you care to stop and think,
You'll find - that so are you!'
We went into a local pub,
The landlord went quite white.
There was a sign, above the bar,
Ghosts only served at night!
Onward to the chippie,
Smell of frying, licked our lips.
The operator looked at us,
Said, 'Boys, you've had your chips!'
The undertaker welcomed us,
Business was rather dead.
He stood perplexed and puzzled,
'We've met before,' he said!
The shock was just too much for him,
For he collapsed and died.
We joined him in the hearse that day,
And all went for a ride!
Now if you think these ramblings,
Come from a tortured mind.
In truth of course, we've all moved on,
To somewhere quite divine!

T G Bloodworth

ALL ABOUT YOU - PART ONE

So you think you're secure
In that person you hide
And no one but no one
Can perceive what's inside
I'll tell you a secret
If you promise to keep it
You're ever so ever so
Wrong

All life is based on two primary factors
Reproduction and self-preservation
The latter
Is your will to survive
The former
Release and frustration
You're merely an extension of both
An electrobiochemical neural compilation

The style of your hair
The make-up you wear
The turn of your head
How you sit in a chair
The way that you stand
Or talk with your hands
Are simply awaiting
Another's command
The arch of your back
The wrinkles and cracks
That grin or that grimace
You give
Or you lack

From your heels to your head
You're so easily read
You're openly heard
Yet you've not
Said a word
There's so much to be told
About you
That you'll just have to wait
For part two

Mark Anthony Noble

YESTER YOU

Would you recognise
The face you had
Before they took
Your money
Or have you become
A stranger to yourself?

Would you know you
If you met you
Before you crossed
The street
To find your demons
On the other side?

Would you understand
A single word
The yester you
Was saying
Or can you only hear
The sound of sorrow's choir?

Rod Trott

OPERATOR

What do we mean by the term *operator*?
It might be the one who we ask for a number,
Who works in the building where telephones ring.
It might be the fireman, the farmer, the plumber
Who operates engines, tractors and bring
Repairs to those pipes once leaking and bursting.
The man with the camera who operates scenes
For viewing on TV, for weddings just thirsting
To capture the joy that special day means.
It might be the surgeon who's skilled in the theatre
Removing the cause of so much disease:
But the great operator of all creation
Holds this world in His hands, will not cease
From loving and making the sunrise and sunset,
Forgiving all those who kneel at His feet
In contrite repentance; this great operator
Wants all of His children to truly be healed
Of sins that cause suffering because of not listening
To the voice operating with love, joy and peace.

Marion Skelton

THE DAY

Was asked at three pm to go forward patrol
Corporal Jones and five others were told enrol
The tin bangers they threw when we were close
As we raced to our holes, bullets feared most.
Could see fresh soil where they had laid mines
So real speed and care became embed in minds.

John J Flint

A Day In The Life Of A Hospital Patient

The breakfast cart comes clattering in,
Filled with 'delights', which belong in a bin!
Tea or coffee in a plastic cup,
Weak and lukewarm, you need to drink it up.

Is that the time? It's nearly eight,
And I've still got 27 pills to take!
'Take them all at once,' a nurse suggests,
They'll probably take all day to digest!

The newspaper trolley arrives on the ward,
Just as the doctors walk through the doors.
Wearing hipster jeans and belly button rings,
When did doctors become such young trendy things?

Suddenly you hear your name being called,
And you're off to X-ray, just down the hall.
Out of X-ray in five minutes flat,
Then a two hour wait, until someone can take you back!

2pm and your visitors arrive,
And ask how you have been, you answer, 'Just fine.'
'Where were you cut, and can we see?'
'How many stitches?' they ask gleefully.

'We're off now,' your visitors say,
And promise to visit another day,
Peace and quiet now you finally think,
Oh no! It's time for another warm drink.

Not long until hot chocolate is served,
And definitely the best thing in hospital I've heard.
Snuggling down to try to sleep,
Something is flickering so you take a peek,
The main ward light is in need of repair,
The end of a restful day in hospital care!

Gail McPherson

LOVESICK

I'm tired and I'm weak
But I still can't sleep
I know it's sick and it's wrong
But I keep on thinking you're the one
I'm sad and I'm blue
But I just want to be with you
I can't think straight any more
But I still want to be your whore

You act like you don't care
And yet you know I'm still out there

You're special and you're fine
And I hope that you're still mine
You're stubborn just like me
And you just, drive me crazy

We have to work this out
Just both stop messing about
We can make this relationship work
Just stop being a jerk
We can put the past behind us, and live together again
Just want to know, because really it's simply a case of when.

Jenna Lisa Devonald

UN ESPRIT CASSÉ

Within a faceless entourage
There's one who suffers most
A spirit torn asunder
Who loved and cared the most

A heart that dies along with yours
A passion unfulfilled
Squandered opportunities
Suppressed by strangers, killed

A single rose to say goodbye
Regrets to haunt, so cold
The vision of your countenance
Never to grow old

What's life, but pain and anguish?
Tempered by sweet dreams
Never reaching fruitfulness
Condemned by wild extremes

As your tortured soul finds freedom
This love, so pure and brave
Will yearn for you, and daily pray
We'll meet, beyond the grave.

John Robinson

A THOUSAND MILES AWAY

A thousand miles away and worlds apart;
Yet joined in sadness, loss and tragedy.
A million lives destroyed at Asia's heart,
When death came rolling in from far at sea.

When warning tremors shook that secret ground,
Beneath the earth and water, no one knew.
No chance, no clue was given, not a sound,
To warn the world that death was passing through.

So many precious lives were washed away.
So deep the sorrow felt both near and far.
So much been said but nothing left to say,
To mourners asking where their loved ones are.

The sun was shining brightly in the sky.
The trees were swaying gently in the breeze.
The question in a billion minds is, 'Why?'
So much destruction came from quiet seas.

A thousand miles away we sit and grieve,
For people who, not known to us, lay still;
And many who they've left behind, bereaved,
To face each day must summon iron will.

A thousand miles away, I sit and pray,
For those who, burned with agony, remain.
That light may guide them through their darkest day,
And fill them with the strength to start again.

Natasha Jules

ANOTHER DAY INSIDE

7am, on this cold winter morn
The ominous buzz of the light
Descends upon the dorm.

Immediately, I'm awake
And my chest grows tight
Through sheer fright
Of what another long day inside
Could bring.

We line up for breakfast
And play our favourite game
'How many 'roaches can we kill?'
In a perverse way, it keeps us sane
And eases the pain of always being ill
Thanks to those kitchens
I'd not feed a dog in.

Next, it's off to work I go
Buffeting the floors
Boredom eased, by reading the obscene graffiti
Scrawled upon the cold grey walls.

Thankfully today passes quickly
After 'association', it's back to the dorm
And after the usual flurry of boredom-fuelled half-hearted punches
Some bed-tipping too
I escape into sleep
And dream of home
And you.

Russ Hyman

THE ELECTRIC STORM

Wind bellowed with its tremendous roar,
'Rain come quickly, give it some more!
Spread your wet blanket, cause lots of damage,
Mix in some acid, for we're on a rampage.
I'll whip through the trees, give it my all,
Pound down some buildings, watching them fall.
Shaking scenery, making it dance,
Scattering rubbish, taking no chance
For I am the wizard of weather.

Lightning strike down, cause utter destruction,
See that down there, slice through that construction.
I have the power, nothing stands in my way.
Everything surrender or you will soon pay.
I am the demon of the night.
I'm indestructible, shattering everything in sight.
I sit stirring weather in my cauldron in the sky,
Interfere and you will die,
For I am the wizard of weather!'

Linda Benson

PLANET EARTH

The moon gently sleeps
Above the broken images of yesterdays so bright
It's like this witch with old age is weakened
Somewhere the trees have no life.
Candlelights they burn through tomorrow
They light an empty house down on the bed
Soon the seas will seek them
The wind whispers no
It will be the last.

Mark Roberson

YOU ARE

You are
>> The sparkle in a diamond,
>> The bubbles in champagne,
>> The magic in the music,
>> The rainbow after rain.

You are
>> The bliss in a kiss,
>> The high in all the lows,
>> The rhyme and the rhythm,
>> The scent of the tuberose.

You are
>> The buzz in a party,
>> The wind in my sails,
>> The wonder in my thoughts,
>> My shelter from the gales.

You are the treasure that I love.

Margaret Nixon

TIME AFTER TIME

It happens every year, it seems,
>> fire and flame on whins
That leave burned-black witches' fingers
>> touching on light and senses.
Probing above the ground warm and hissing
>> they cool in winter's snowflake
Saturnine beauty, scented with earthiness,
>> deep-rooted far below and forever.

John Michael Doherty

IF I COULD

If I could glimpse into Heaven
And witness all its glory
I could sit and write you
A fascinating story
I could write about the angels
Who float on calming air
I could write about family members
Who left and travelled there
I could tell you how they fare
In the Almighty's golden home
I could tell you what they do
And where they go to roam
I could bring you all the comfort
And also bring release
I could help to ease your grief
And put your mind at peace
But since I cannot get beyond
The darkened deep blue sky
I'll have to stay on Earth
And sit and wonder why.

Steven Wilson

ARTIFICIAL FLAVOURING

We stuff our faces
in remembrance of the fallen
and as our mouths drop open
in goes artificial flavouring.

And we think of our deliverers
and of what they died for
and of how we have honoured them
in our lives and in our eating.

Peter Asher

WING TUNG

She's gorgeous with a little sweet mouth
her facial expression looks like mine

How clever she is
she looks at me
tries to read my lips
and follow my words
'Good, good, good morning'

She does not want to sleep yet
she likes to talk to me
listens to my words

She is not comfortable
hungers for milk
wants to pee
or just moody

Let me talk to her
she becomes quiet
and listens to me
talks to me
then we smile and even laugh

It's really hard
to leave her for the airport
she must come to England
to study and live with me

At least she'll ring my number
when her little fingers are ready
and we'll talk and talk
again and again

Come, come here
my little angel

Mei Yuk Wong

OUTREACH

Birth
Marriages are made in Heaven
but must be lived on Earth.
Bodies in love create spirits
in harmony. Babies born
are miracles to love and to cherish.

Life
The flotsam and jetsam of living
easily dispersed. Each wave,
by the moon controlled,
ebb and flow rhythms
soothe and make breathing itself
a lyric for life.

Scenario
He stood in wonder
at the girl asleep.
She sighed -
rose no more a maiden.
When of age the child
unlocked the door:
the world was blessed.

Gift
The man didn't tell us
his name: we didn't ask.
It seemed irrelevant,
as when he left
nothing had changed.
Our uniqueness is
the substance of our being.

Michael Fenton

OBSESSIVE OBSESSIONS

It's time to start afresh - they say,
We must shed excess pounds,
To be again, a svelte size 10
Will turn those frowns around!

Exercise is what we need
To combat wobbly thighs,
We need to sweat, and don't forget
It's 'fatties' men despise.

With compliments! A diet sheet
So each and every day,
They stipulate what's on your plate
To keep the weight at bay.

And all that water they suggest
Ensures that constantly
We're overdue to use the loo
To be a better 'me'.

The magazines are full of ways
To make this nation slim
But what about the ones without
The wish to join a gym?

It seems to me we overlook
The curvy fuller figure,
Accentuate the 'perfect 8'
And disregard the bigger.

My friend has got bulimia
And I know who to blame,
A world obsessed with 'thin is best'
Has caused her eating shame.

Kelly Sibley

THROUGH THE EYES OF A SOLDIER

As I'm standing guard on this front line
My heart and life is not Thine
In this world which is no longer divine
I pray to the Lord above to send some peace and love
Down from Heaven above.

My heart is pounding, faster and faster
As I see innocent lives taken before my eyes
And left just to die.

I often ask the Lord above, why
And what has happened to that thing called love?

I most certainly don't like what I see, day by day
But as I stand here on this front line
Guarding and defending this world,
Which was created for Thine.

I see plenty of bloodshed, killings, bombings, death,
Hatred and tears, many men, women and children
Running, 'cause their lives are in fear every day.
Buildings collapsing all around me as they're hit by bombs,
People's bodies flying from one to the other
But what can one do -
When loads of others don't even have a clue?

So think of me here, fighting for peace in our world today,
And all those many families that don't get the chance
To face life, day by day

This isn't easy here any day of my life, but someone
Has to defend this world which is being destroyed for no reason
Or choice of mine.

Think of me every day as I give you a preview of this world today,
Through my eyes as a soldier
I pray that my angels are always on my shoulder.
Guarding and defending me as I fight here on this front line
To save this world which was created many years ago
Out of peace and love from God above.

Anastasia Williams Cowper

SOLUTION?

Oh! Stick limbed child with swollen belly,
Why do they show you on the telly?
With washboard ribs and hopeless eyes,
Nose and mouth a-crawl with flies.
Nothing childlike, nothing bold,
Just the death wait of the old.
Lips shrunk back in a skeleton grin,
The harvest of a sick world's sin.

Must they show the price we pay,
For going our 'I'm OK Jack' way?
'Turn it off Dear, we're all right,
Our little darlings are tucked up tight,
So dry your eyes, I'll do you proud,
Things like that shouldn't be allowed,
Come, get your coat and I'll take you out,
For a T-bone steak and a bottle of stout.'

Dennis Chancellor

MY PHOTOGRAPHS

I feel the way I look in my photographs
And wonder why I can't get more alarmed
There's reasons for some outcomes in those photographs
For people that I've met and left uncharmed

That awkward move affected and self-conscious
You know the thoughts that brought them to appear
You see it when you ponder on your photograph
And cringe to think the world sees what is there

That was not a good day when they took my photograph
I was grossly overweight and feeling blue
If she took it now I'm sure I'd look much better -
Let's cut the crap I know that's just not true

For through the years and loads and loads of pictures
It's a trick of light when they are any good
Just when I think I'm getting better looking
The next photo shows a lump of suet pud

Raymond Barber

DREADED DEMONS

Demoralising dope demands, draining determination
Demons decisions dictate delirium,
Distress demonstrating doom
Dragged deep down darkening dungeons
Dangerous dragons, dissenting deceivers,
Delaying distant discriminations developing
Decent departure deprived devouring devastation.
Distorted details deform, divulged diversion
Disobedient disarray denying detour
Decadent desires defy dreams.

Elaine Priscilla Kilshaw

MILLIENIELLE (OR THE SONNET)

Instead of words to pictures framed,
Verbal Picasso at his worst,
Displays a phonic manic burst,
Careless how the impact's aimed.
And scatters scraps of worried prose,
Together tossed, unscanned, unrhymed,
In half-dissected thoughts to show,
The measure of a challenged mind.

In garbled text a message writ,
The harried jigsaw on a page,
Assaults the mind and curbs the wit,
Or moved a soul to senseless rage.
At dissonance of life made clear,
Which charms not neither does it cheer.

Peggy Sinclair

REMEMBER

Proud men and women, old and young
Head held high
Marching past the Cenotaph
Honouring the dead
The bugle sounds its haunting tune
Silence
Until it's heard again
And all around, a field of blood-red poppies
Come alive on a cold November morn
As the old comrades fade away
Will the next generation of today
Remember?

Teresa R Chester

BARRIERS

Pent-up anger
Fear of life
Times of joy
Times of strife.
Bearing daily
All our fears,
Smiles and laughter
Turned to tears.

Staring blindly
At the sky,
Watching time
Go slowly by.
Hardly share
A word or two,
What is this life
If not with you?

Sit at home
Watch TV
Words and pictures
Brainwash me.
Cartoons, movies
Warm my heart
Another day
Another start.

John Foley

FREE

World spinning,
nothing moves,

Why is it that these rough things soothe?

The drugs, they hit,
which is a good thing?
They are bad for you
but apparently that's 'bling'.

To feel good
you have to know bad.
That's sad,
which means I can be happy?

Alcoholics are depressed
and alcohol is a depressive?
Then why is it at the end of a long day
I need a beer, to cheer me up? Am I obsessive?
Which then means,
I don't need to obsess?
Is this backward walk
the only way to progress?
Am I lost in this world
of none that ain't found
or am I let loose in these chains
unbound?

Chris Berry

SNAKE

This snake so green, like the
Jealousy, in his deadpan eyes.
Tongue, hissing and forked,
Shoots out to me like lies.
Coiled and twisted, stretched his
Body long, like his ego.
This snake so venomous, wounding,
Like the man I know should go.

Go, go back to that place, that
You came slithering from.
Take with you your hissing, lying
Tongue, and unbending thumb.
Your cruel, and dangerous nature,
Snake is what you'll be forever.
My love, my heart shrivelled, died,
Like the breaking of a shooting star.

Jean Neville

SICK OF . . .

Sick of the thoughts,
Sick of the fury,
Running in my being,
Control is going,
Tiredness is taking over,
Weakening me by the hour,
But the fury don't dissolve,
Cannot control the power,
In my being,
Don't want to,
Want to let go.
Sick of waiting, to be hunted.

Faneela Bi

Past, Present And Future

'Forget the past -
Live the present,
And shape the future'
Is what my mother
Keeps telling me
Forever and ever!

Do you believe this?
Tell me my friend
Can you ever bring -
The past to an end?
I always kept thinking this,
When finally I got a solution
I know now it's not just some intuition.

Yes it is true the past can never,
Be brought to an end.
For it is what has
Already once happened.
It cannot be brought to an end
For it itself is the end.

Then why spend time over
What has already ended?
Why not think how it can be mended?
This will form our present -
And if it be bright,
The future will not be spent
In sadness or in fright.

For when the present will one day end
The future will always on it depend!

Pravi Prakash

A BLACKBIRD'S FOND FAREWELL

With blanket approach
As the threatening gloom of winter's darkening veil
Spreads cautiously across the dismal sky
And nothing seems to matter,
What now can brighten lives?
Then suddenly a sound of uplifting musical charm
An enchanting repertoire of sheer delight,
As if a messenger with persuasive notes
Was designed to bewitch dreary lives by chance.
Now the music, with crescendo, fills the air
As ears absorb an experience of delight,
An expressive blackbird so clearly in view
Rehearsing well, with vocal chords, so fine,
Seemingly hoping that all listeners
Should witness now, this final show.
'No curtain call',
Bidding now his audience 'a musical goodnight'
Bows out so gracefully
And disappears 'neath darkening skies,
From sight.

Irene Grahame

SILENCE

Not a single soul shall cry for me
Nor weep at my demise; no tear shall ever wet the cheek
Of those who smirk, behind laughing eyes
All that did distort my life
Did together concede my fate, voiceless whispers swiftly say
This lost boy left us forever today
Silence is all to be heard here now
Naught but the fantastic still
Remember me for the good
The imaginary life that we created
Masquerading as what we weren't
To fulfil our dreams of peace
Well, sometimes we just can't have that hope
That love is all we see, we can't pretend forever
That this life could easily be
Perfection. I leave this world with memories
Of me and my infinite scars
Then tell me that you care
Underneath my glowing star.
I'm sorry . . .

Catherine Palin

THE SLUG

Under a lichen-covered stone
In a world of its own
Out of the light of day
The slug whiles his time away
Emerging at sundown to foil
Efforts of all who till the soil
Voraciously devouring both
Roots and succulent young growth
On cultivated plants it feeds
Preferable to common weeds
Aphids black and white
Scab mildew and blight
Gardeners eradicate any bug
But the invulnerable slug
Pellets that they strew galore
Kill the slugs' natural predator
The hedgehog takes in the bait
From the slugs that it ate
Leaving the slug to prevail
With assistance from his mate the snail
A row of beans, looking good
Are overnight nipped in the bud
To guess the culprit you can't fail
He leaves behind a silver trail
It seems we can't escape
These strips of living sellotape
They are just as nature planned
Not to be held in the hand
And then, you might say
Man is slimy, in a different way.

Vic Calladine

AN ANGEL BY MY SIDE

I have an angel by my side
I always know she's there
She never lets me down
But lets me know she cares
When some things get too much
And I don't know where to turn
It's then I feel my angel's touch
She keeps me free from harm
I never have the need to worry
For I know she's by my side
And in this life of hurry
She eases my bumpy ride
I might feel a gentle stroke
Like a feather against my face
Or maybe just a little poke
At just the right time or place
I might see numbers on my clock
As I wake up during the night
The numbers are my messages
So I must always get them right
Sometimes the phone will ring
But on the line there is no sound
I know it's the work of my angel
Letting me know that she's around
Whichever way she comes to me
I always sit up and take note
For all that she is really doing
Is making sure that I can cope.

Margaret Ward

AN ANGEL'S DISTRESS

An asylum a-blazing with agony
Tears are shedding on cheeks
Some are counting their seconds
Some are shivering with results
Those who are not freed from illness or injury
They are in deep rest of sleep
Doctor has treated with full efforts
As a negotiator to relieve from disease
To bring back his function of life span
White swans are jazzing around sufferers
Plaster over with an intimacy, posing bountiful words
Surgery to morbid organs to increase period of time
Those who are dangling to close their account.
Their orison to almighty may forgive to some livings
Even, they are unsuccessful at their medical exam
They cry out in their hearts in a pitiful manner
They are mediators between Hell and Heaven.
In a contingency procedure of life
To their ails has no certain treatment.
They are ordinary human beings; even they are angels
To flick up pains and distress from human life.

She is an angel, loyal to sick cases
She smiles brightly with gracious words
But she caught an incurable disease
Her life story switched with some viral infection
As a virus, husband afflicts with flaming behaviour
With forbearance, she boldly stitched it on her body
To relieve her from distress, there's no certain vaccine
Her dreams bolt down by her partner, without mercy
Her psychogenic condition losing self-assurance
Trust with a fifty-fifty, she made herself a surgical operation
Without any anaesthesia, without any operating theatre

Her hubby virus caught her mental imbalances
Can post mortem be the answer to her deep sleep?
Even her bodily functional conditions are healthy
It's a death toll to her unending lifeline

Bollimuntha Venkata Ramana Rao

PRAYER FLAGS

They were there again today
The poly bags flapping in the wind
Branches holding them aloft
Prayer flags for the dead.
The stark tree trunks of winter
Putting their arms out in sorrow
To support these messages of mourning.
We don't forget our loved ones
We don't need these symbols of death.
The loss is ever present
Painful reminders cut deep
We need no reminders of death.
Rethink the symbolism
View the scene with joy
In hope that the leaves and blossom
Will dispel our sorrow
In manifestation of love and joy.

Joan R Gilmour

PRESERVING THE MONARCHY

'After you with the flu, Your Majesty,
Well Ma'am, you did miss the point!'

Will good Queen Elizabeth come under attack
    Since missing the flu jab, protection did lack?
Sojourning in Aberdeenshire, at Balmoral grand,
    The necessary vaccine was not close to hand;
Like all of her subjects, aged sixty-five plus,
    The Queen takes the flu jab without any fuss,
Knowing full well, the health benefits it brings,
    The vaccine is taken without any strings.

On a previous occasion, when the bug was about,
    When contracting influenza, she could not go out,
Her public engagements were then sadly curtailed,
    Because her resistance had miserably failed;
There is nothing worse when eyes and nose run,
    And continually sneezing is not any fun.
The ache in the head and the back is severe,
    When all you can do is just persevere.

But like a good leader, the example was set,
    Although the flu vaccine she had not had yet,
By raising her sleeve and baring an arm,
    Accepting the vaccine prevented alarm;
Now like the rest of the sixty-fives plus,
    Her Majesty can say, 'I'm now one of us!'
Her health is protected from the dreaded flu strain,
    And threats to her health no longer remain.

So long live Her Majesty, in continued good health,
    Something more valuable than having great wealth,
Long over England may she continually reign,
    And our British monarchy let no one disdain;

With each passing year, may her health hold full strong,
    By which we'll all know that nothing is wrong,
Remembering also, that whenever it's due -
    Having the vaccine, prevents having flu!

'Just making a point, Ma'am' Ahem!

Edward James Williams
A Bystander Poet

AUSCHWITZ

They rest in millions beneath the soil
Robbed of life by fellow human beings
By individuals who were consumed
With hatred and prejudice,
Bigotry and intolerance,
Spite and fanaticism.

Innocent, defenceless children,
Women and men, young and old,
Oppressed, persecuted, humiliated,
Tortured, tormented and subdued,
By a corrupt, depraved, ruthless regime.

The perpetrators of the cruelty are gone
But Auschwitz remains, hallowed ground,
A monumental mausoleum, to the memory
Of all who perished, a place of pilgrimage
For those who survived, a stern warning
For all humankind.

Liam Heaney

REMEMBRANCE SUNDAY

At 11 o'clock, on the 11th November day,
Old comrades stand in proud array,
Many remember the two world wars,
And speak so sadly about what they saw.

The poppy is traditionally the fallen dead,
But old comrades remember them alive instead,
Don't ever forget those who fought,
And with their help, this country was safely brought.

Brought through the worst of living *Hell,*
And many a terrible tale old comrades will tell,
But they live on proud in name,
Let's hope we never see war in this country again.

Let's not forget what it really does mean,
Ask any old comrade, and they say where they've been,
Medals shining in the bright sunlight,
May God bless them and keep them safe and alright.

Barbara Holme

HENRY

They make fun of Henry, but never in public
Laughing behind his back whenever he turns
Always in groups and never alone
Careful, very careful never to upset him
Gracious and caring when one on one
They know he is different to them

Henry is happy when he is surrounded
Mouthing words that mean little, to friends that mean less
Showing courage and candour through blind eyes
Unaware of his disadvantage, oblivious to those who mock
Caring only for attention and recognition
Believing he is just like them

Humorous, sometimes, yet unintentionally so
Sincerity passing over those who continually mock
Used as an afterthought and plaything for most
Earning respect through persistence, an impossibility
Refusing bluntly to be discarded as an outsider
Unlike them, he is special.

Alan Zoltie

MY AIM IS TRUE

'My aim is true,'
Said the fish that was snagged.
'What a beauty!'
Outstretched hands had bragged.
'My aim is true,'
Said the fish, as he writhed from bank to net.
'Wife, look at the size of this!'
Said the fisherman firing up the skillet.
'My aim is true,'
Said the fish as he eyed the searing pan.
'Fetch the tartar sauce,'
Said the stout, salivating fisherman.
'My aim is true,'
Said the fish as he exhaled his last breath.
'I think food poisoning,'
Said the coroner, of the fisherman's death.

Peter Abarney

MY DEAR DEPARTED OLD CATS

I look up into the sky and I can see
My dear old cats looking down on me
They float on the clouds so high above
Into a garden of paradise of everlasting love.
I miss and grieve for them day after day
But I know God cares for them in every way
In a wondrous place where angels fly.
Their wings so radiant light up the sky,
When I feel sad, in the clouds I see them play
As they drift along, they seem to say
'Don't be sad, we are always here too,
We are your guardian angels looking down on you.'

Christine Munton

ALL FOR NOTHING

Dead bodies,
Missing limbs,
Broken hearts,
Haunting, staring faces.
Demolished homes,
Devastated lives.
No one to rebuild places.
Barbed wire and no go zones,
All refuse to find some common ground.
Loved ones lost and never found.
Lives are cheap
No respect for others.
Wounds so deep,
No one cares for my brothers,
Both killed.
Power thirsty leaders, obviously thrilled
Convince themselves it's in the name of God
As the gravediggers turn the next sad sod.

J W Whiteacre

DON'T GO OUT TONIGHT!

Bats streak,
Across a silver moon,
Hanging in a freezing sky,
Black cats stalk
Amongst crumbling tombs
Cheap lucky rings
Afford no protection
On this night
As old towers
Strike off the hours
Don't go out tonight!
On Hallowe'en.

Paul Wilkins

ME BUCKET!

Me best friend is me bucket,
    Cos when I'm ill it's by me side,
And when I'm playing hide 'n' seek,
    It's where I like to hide.
It's filled me many water guns,
    Earned me money washing the car,
It's stood for many a goal post,
    And has helped collect frogs from afar.
It's held tickets in the raffle,
    And sand in the lucky dip,
It's travelled in the minibus,
    When I went on me school trip.
And when we all went camping,
    I took me bucket, thinking ahead,
Cos sometimes when I'm away from home,
    I occasionally wet me bed.
Me bucket is me special friend,
    Cos it never groans or teases,
It's always around when I need it,
    And never goes off when it pleases.
I've used it for me fishin',
    And taken it to school,
Even if me mates think I'm daft,
    They think me bucket's cool!

Tony Pratt

MAKE-OVER

They dwelt in a hovel in Tooting Bec,
With failed DIY and an outside loo,
Abysmally furnished, a dreary wreck,
Till the TV team showed what it could do.
Now bus loads of tourists confirm it must
Come potentially under the National Trust.

The long-haired consultant with lace jabots
And velveteen weskit looked askance
At the MFI fittings. They had to go,
Replaced by *objets,* exotic plants,
Ionic pilasters and - notion peachy -
An atrium with a bust of Nietzsche.

Other TV experts, gardening creatures,
Attacked the yard, knocked down the shed,
Installed a ha-ha, some water features,
Dug up the sprouts and built instead
A gazebo with panoramic view
In lieu of the clapped-out barbecue.

At the height of the property boom, they sold
And - thanks to more TV advice,
On buying abroad - their pot of gold
Went far. Now chatelaines of a rather nice
Palladian palazzo near Assisi
They tend their vineyards and take life easy.

Norman Bissett

ZEEBRUGGE - 1987

Four sailors ran a ferry boat across the briny deep,
To speed the people on their holidays.
Their names were 'Someone', 'Everyone', No one' and 'Anyone'.
They did their separate jobs, their separate ways.

The shutting of the boat's bow doors, a most important job,
Was one in which each sailor played a part.
They each took turns to do it in a rota of some kind
And that was where the trouble seemed to start.

'Everyone' thought 'Someone' would have shut the door that day,
Though 'Anyone' could do it, 'No one' did.
'Someone' then swore blind that 'Everyone' should be the one,
But 'Everyone' threw tantrums like a kid!

'Anyone' could do it, 'Everyone' cried in disgust,
But 'No one' realised it would not be done.
So off the ferry trundled, mouth wide open to the sea,
And sank, just as its journey had begun.

Some people lost their luggage, some people lost their cars,
Some people lost their lives, their families too,
And 'Everyone' blamed 'Someone', because 'No one' went and did
What 'Anyone' should have the sense to do!

Mick Nash

THE WAITING ROOM

Ashen faces, legs in braces, pimples large and small
Arms in slings and sundry things affecting one and all
Hacking coughs and sneezing kids, people with ill-fitting wigs
Eyes with patches, knees with bruises, injections for exotic cruises,
Pregnant mums with fattened tums awaiting natal checks
Men with back-lash, sitting rigid, collar braces supporting necks
Measles, mumps and laryngitis, mundane things that don't excite us
Diabetes, tonsils, trauma, stomachs with some odd disorder
Bunions, boils, mumps and bumps, amputees with just a stump
Dracula nurse in room thirteen waiting for your blood
sticking in the needle further than she should
always saying 'A little scratch' but really this is just a catch
she doesn't mean a scratch at all, she means a prick, but protocol
demands she use the scratch word now cos
                    'Little Prick' they won't allow
There's flu injections for the old, Aspirin for just a cold
Counselling for those in need, diet advice for too much feed
Chiropody for aching feet, go on try, it works a treat,
Headache, backache, shingles, piles, best selection around for miles
The buzzer buzzes, they all look up to see their doctor's name light up
they hold their numbers in their hand, engraved on plastic,
                                which they hang
on a designated hook before they go, to see their chosen medico.

John Gilbert Slade

THINK TWICE

Fighting over religion,
What a waste of time and life.
Praying to unseen gods
Seems to cause more wars and strife.
I do not question, our souls live on
Once we die and our bodies are gone.
Perhaps we meet our Maker one day
And that will be the time to pray.
To look back and account for all our sins,
To see our mistakes and our wrong doings.
Think twice dear folk, before you kill
Because we were told this is against God's will.
If cruel and unkind, we will pay the price,
If not while on Earth
Then in the next life!

G Maynard

SILVER AND GOLD

Lashings of silver
Settings of gold
Water clear crystal
Walls precious stone

A lover calling
Mysteries unfold
Celestial bride unveiling
Ancient secrets told

Eternity revealing
A new dawn
Blind eyes seeing
Lovesick hearts yearn no more.

Emma Akuffo

BEHIND THE MASK

I am drifting aimlessly as a cloud
Way above earthly things
Up, up and beyond sight or sound
Of creatures small and birds that sing.
In a world of my own, my life cut short
As I am listless and forlorn
Though faintly aware that I have been saved
and brought to port
Nevertheless I would that I be gone:
It is difficult to come to terms
With what I am and have become
I as that of a worm will never turn
Shall always remain the same when day is done.

Endlessly my life is one roundabout and swings
Swinging above the same old ground
Would that I was different - hence I fling
All care to the wind for I no longer want to be around;
The goodness of those who surround me
Am undeserving of their care and concern
If they knew me as my siblings see
They would scorn and spurn.
For I am unfit to walk this Earth
Hence I drift aimlessly as a cloud
Way above earthly things
Up, up and beyond sight or sound
Of creatures small and birds that sing.

Elizabeth Constable Scott

A GLIMPSE OF HEAVEN

Fingers tangled
in my hair.
Chest against mine,
strong and bare.

Pulling me closer,
lips find yours.
Soft and gentle,
never a pause.

Skin touching,
white and black.
Hands sliding
down your back.

Feel you against me,
hardness and heat.
Breath on my face,
rapid heartbeat.

Reaching deeply,
insatiable thirst.
Moving, feeling,
until we burst.

Quiet, peaceful,
liquids seep.
Close together
we fall asleep.

Gillian L Bestwick

THE SCARS OF THE BATTLEFIELD

The seas of white crosses
Tell stories of the brave
In service to country
Their lives they gave.
The red poppy that dances
Amidst fields of green
Reflects rivers of blood
Of war, vile and obscene.
They came to win freedom
For generations to come
Could they really have known
What had to be done?
They left our shores
And travelled afar
To fight for the honour
Of a country at war.
So young, so naive
They all must have been
To witness the bloodshed
Which should never be seen.
And yet the fighting continues
More men have to die
And leave families behind
Who don't understand why.
Oh God, why let it happen
Why have it this way?
The cost of one young life
Is too much to pay!

Tracy Thorogood

WE WILL REMEMBER THEM

We wander freely o'er our land
We should remember and understand
Our brave soldiers went to war
For freedom and for so much more
We will remember them

We see the poppies in the fields
Swaying gently in the breeze
Young men that were oh so brave
Poppies now lie on their grave
We will remember them

So many sons who left their mums
Marching gaily with their chums
They little knew what was in store
Until they faced the blood and gore
We will remember them

Fighting in a foreign land
Trying hard to understand
The daily struggle, conflict and strife
The terrible senseless loss of life
We will remember them

So when we wander o'er our land
Think of the gallant, glorious band
The young men who faced their fears
They gave their lives for our future years
We will remember them

B M Beatson

POPPIES

Flanders' fields of mud and dust
And the ashes of the dead,
Where the poppies that grow as memories
Are tinted by those who bled.

They mature in the sun of a hundred years
And are watered by the tears of wives,
Forever they remain in remembrance
Of so many wasted lives.

Each petal holds within its grasp
The soul of a mother's son,
Who marched to die for freedom's sake
With his helmet and his gun.

No longer do the bugles call
No longer the artillery fire,
No longer do the infantry tread
Across the trenches and the wire.

But we cannot be allowed to forget
The sacrifice that so many made,
In giving their lives for country
Now that their wreaths are laid.

So on the eleventh November day
At the strike of the eleventh hour,
We stand in silence, all as one
To honour the Remembrance flower.

Malcolm Dewhirst

THE WORD IN THE SAND

'What shall we do with this woman of sin?'
They asked, each hand holding a stone.
They hoped that the answer would alley any guilt:
But Jesus, no sin would condone
'Let him without sin, cast the first stone,'
He bent down and wrote in the sand.
They all walked away, the oldest one first
And He brushed the dust with His hand.
With love in His heart, He looked in her eye.
'Has no one condemned you? Neither do I.
Go sin no more,' with a smile He did say.
And with joy in her heart, she went on her way.

He was the Word and He wrote in the sand,
And the power of His Word forever will stand.

Patrick P McCarthy

COMRADES

A platoon of soldiers set foot on a foreign shore,
Alas many a one would see their home no more.
The sea moved swiftly across the sand,
Sand soon to mingle with the blood of man,
Ten, twenty, fifty, sixty.
Since that history day time has passed quickly.

2004, once more old soldiers meet on that shore, and recall,
The conflict and brothers, who on that beach did fall.
Now frail veterans are silent beneath the sun so bright,
They gaze at that monument, a symbol for everything right,
Suddenly brave men have tears in their eye,
They've heard a bugle play *The Last Goodbye!*

John A Booth

THANK YOU DAD

I was only a child of three or four
when Daddy told us about the war
I thought then in my childish way
why didn't you make it all go away?
Then little by little he told us more
felt we should know, what had gone before
how men had fought and died for peace
in hope that future wars would cease.
A peaceful time for you and me
to live with pride and dignity.
My father died aged forty-five
six kids he left to survive.
We are the lucky ones I think
as Dad's ship didn't sink
it wasn't bombed or blown apart
he lived to tell us from the heart
so that we'd grow but not forget
soldier, sailor, airman, forever in your debt.
So it is with pride, I wear your flower -
on the eleventh day of the eleventh month of the eleventh hour.

Brenda Birchall

GOD'S LOVE

Flowers of all descriptions
In different shapes and size
Extend their little petals
And reach up to the skies

To catch the falling raindrops
Descending from above
A gift from God in Heaven
Sent with all His love.

Ken Mulligan

SILENT EMOTIONS

She glides in effortless motion,
Melting all admirers,
Where hearts, meeting at the tapered steps,
Are in tune with her radiant smile;
Beckoning the soft cheeks of love's kisses,
Calling a thousand names,
On lips traced by every man, dearly to impart.
Pearl white beads, jewel her picture,
Courteous to the framed hopes and minds,
Whispering in the fragile air,
Sweeter than fruitful eyes,
Devouring life's efforts.
Sensuous fingers, existing only in dreams,
Caress with each hair,
As the bosom of captivity,
Hangs in the depths of imagination,
Praying on the shadowless breath.
Aside, voiceless wings envelop heavenly,
Curves of the hour glass shape of time,
Slipping through a moment of eternities.

Christopher W Wolfe

THOSE GENTLE HANDS

(This poem was written for and is dedicated
to Dr Chris Lincoln - with my sincere gratitude)

The light began to filter through
My poor dazed eyes, as I came to.
Strange figures flittered to and fro -
People whom I did not know.

A heart attack was what they said
Had brought me to an uneasy bed.
The haze then left my fevered brain -
I became my normal self again.

The medics all had done their best,
Now all I had to do was rest.
The surgeon's skill had paved the way
For me to live another day.

His tender touch had soothed away the pain
And brought me back to life again.
A man who will always stand apart -
With those gentle hands that healed my
                wounded heart.

Mary Baird Hammond

LAMENT

At the ripe old age of seventy-four,
I can't remember when
Someone said my allotted span
Was three score years and ten!

It seems that I have rocked the boat,
Had four more years to linger!
But yet, I don't intend to see
The Grim Reaper's pointing finger!

I look around and see my friend,
And she is eighty-three.
So now I'm really hoping
That I'll live as long as she!

So when all is done and dusted,
And the bright light comes into view.
I'll sing with all the angels
And enjoy my life anew!

Greta Gaskin

FEAR

I've crushed many armies, in my day,
and beaten kings and lords,
'How is this?' I hear you say,
for I've no armour, magic or swords.

The strongest being, can be crushed,
the weakest just a fly,
my work sometimes is never rushed,
and some it races by.

I have a hold on all,
none will ever be free,
They come and go to my call,
and bend to the will of me.

I will exist when lives are past,
my spirit is always here,
of my name? I hear you ask,
well, let's just say . . . I'm *fear*.

Adam Poole

FIGHTING THE FLAB

Summer's here,
I give a cheer.

My body I hate,
I must lose weight.

I'd love to be thin,
Not bursting within.

So to get slim,
I join a gym.

This flab I'll fight,
With all my might.

An exercise bike,
Saves me a long hike.

Keeping fit,
Hurts a bit.

Don't talk rot,
It hurts a lot.

I'm in such pain,
I have a sprain.

My diet's planned,
Chocolate's banned.

At the weigh in each week,
I'll soon be fit and sleek.

Life will be a peach,
When I sit on the beach.

With ice cream and chips,
That slides to my hips.

I won't get the hump,
I'll be pleasantly plump.

Summer's here,
I'll try next year!

Rosemary Davies

Today's Fashion

Denims that look scruffy,
Flares that sweep the floor,
Wet and frayed, designer made
Fashion is a bore.
Waist on hips, glossy lips,
Hair, three colours or more,
Peaked with gel that sparkles as well
Getting dressed up, must be a chore.
A jewelled midriff that's never cold,
A coat that's never worn,
Earrings like wheels, stiletto heels
I could go on and on.
I enjoy the young who are so bold
I'm envious because I'm old.
If I was young, I'd do the same
Living it up, treating life as a game.

Cassandra May Poultney

PEACE

Sombre is this place where you rest
White stone flowers in eternal bloom, show your name
Young fresh-faced men in a blighty scene, before your last breath
Cheered away by a weeping crowd, sailed away to a Hell
Ravaged by the tunes of heavy gun, nerves torn as they chewed
                                                    the Earth
Lands dressed with wire to rip and shred
Bodies hang, ragged like leaves at autumn's end
Mud-filled craters etched with blown souls, nothing left
Jagged trenches filled with water, scar the landscape
                                        with mute direction
Whistles shrill the smoke-filled air, one final push for glorious days
Scythed as you struggled to lift from lines of despair
Carried by the wings of courage as guns spewed a stinging venom
Until, the ultimate sacrifice and Heaven wept
Though your loss was not in vain, for freedom was won
The war to end all wars and lesson to be learned of your time,
                                        unwisely said
Each year the poppy blooms, more names to be heard
Always remembered for eternity.

Michael Clenton

REMEMBRANCE DAY

Poppies of red swaying in the wind on a lonely hill,
Scenes of battles, long gone, but memories linger still.
Waterlogged fields that fill this mud drenched land,
As bitter conflicts were being fought, hand to hand.

Generations come with flowers to honour their dead,
Fields of poppies pay their tribute with a carpet of red.
Grim determination can always stop the tide of war,
As friendly persuasion stops the lion's mighty roar.

Young men and women, full of life, carefree and gay,
Gave up their lives for a free world in their yesterday.
So wear your poppy with pride, and march behind the band,
Of sacrifices made in defence, of our green and fertile land.

Rows of white crosses, comrades buried side by side,
Never forget those brave men and women who died.
The sound of the guns have long since drifted away.
Let us pay our respects on this, a memorable day.

Raymond Thomas Edwards

ONLY A THOUGHT AWAY

Happy times with sunshiny haze,
Makes you wistful on remembered days,
Time to stop and reminisce,
Oh lovely days, oh such bliss.
Time to look at photos taken,
Each one capturing a special moment,
Time to laugh and time to stare,
At the antics that beheld us there.
Time to wish with time to share,
Back when days seemed perfect there,
Time to go back whenever we please,
To recall these precious memories.
Just for a little while, whenever we choose,
These wonderful thoughts, never to lose.

Jacqueline Ann Johnston

THE POPPY OF REMEMBRANCE

Oh poppy, humble little poppy
The emblem of resurgent war
Ambivalent emotions your red petals portray
Of the valiant soldiers fighting for the cause.

Oh poppy, noble little poppy
Symbol of our heroic soldiers stand
But must it take forever as we humble, stand together
and pray for cessation of our lands.

Gone are all our yesterdays but all are tomorrows
Must end all the pain, the tears and sorrows
But lest we forget what it means you and me
The humble little poppy, wear it with pride for eternity.

D A Sheasby

DEMPSEY

I know it isn't easy to ignore my big brown eyes
I'm a bouncy furry bundle who will soon be quite a size
Labradors grow steadily and at a fair old pace
I need a good sized garden with lots of open space
I'm sure I'll try your patience until I settle down
Remember I'm not human
Just a canine clown.

I'll eat you out of house and home given half a chance
And if you shirk my morning walk, I'll lead a merry dance
Of course I like the summer, but one thing you can bet
There's nothing quite like mud and rain, I may convert you yet!
My annual visit to the vet will cost a tidy fee
You'll see a very different side of life
Now that you have me.

You didn't really have a clue when you took me on
So off we went to classes to learn Sit, Stay, Leave and Come
But that didn't stop me doing all those other things I love
Like pulling washing from the line and running off with gloves
Not what you expected with my pedigree
Think of all that fun you missed
Don't say you disagree.

Now I'm over ten years old and slightly more sedate
Until some poor marauding cat dares venture on our gate
I know you think I'm special, I have my name in print
Always an opportunist, my eyes still have that glint
You'll need to be one jump ahead, if I can suggest
I may be only canine
But I'm streaks above the rest.

Judith MacBeth

DREAMING

When I was young I longed to have a cottage with a view
A rocky path, a gurgling stream, an apple tree or two.
An old stone wall, a faded thatch would grow up from the earth
A rambling rose, a lupine blue would flourish in the turf.

The house itself would welcome all, a sanctuary in a storm
With comfy chairs and roaring fires, alight to keep you warm.
In summertime the sun would stream amidst the leaded lights
Its rosy beams would wend their way to hidden depths and heights.

The birds would mate and sing with joy within the verdant trees
And on the flowers both rich and ripe, drips pollen for the bees.
A lazy cat with fish in mind, strolls down towards the stream
With artful gaze and watchful eye, content to sit and dream.

The languid dog lays in the sun, annoyed by buzzing flies
Does stretch and grunt and flap a paw across his weary eyes.
But wait a while, for here I am upon a bed so soft
Drinking in the summer scents, which over me do waft.

How did I get from child to man with all my heart's desire
I'm here at last, surrounded by the summer's blessed fire.
I laugh out loud, I sing, I dance, a happy trance like state
I have my dream, this is my life, abandoned to my fate.

Muriel Nicola Waldt

BE AT PEACE WITH KUAN YIN, FOREVER MERCIFUL

(Kuan Yin is the goddess of compassion and mercy)

When life seems too hard to bear,
When the world seems so very harsh,
When you're full of worries and no one seems to care,
You know I'm here, please, please just ask.

When you cry an ocean full of tears,
When you feel the pain will never cease,
When you face your demons and release your fears,
You will know you're loved, I will bring you peace.

When you realise your life is a journey,
When the light shines through the broken clouds,
When you understand you will never be lonely,
You will find your faith as I lift the shroud.

When you feel pure unconditional love,
When life is appreciated through good and bad,
When you absorb the knowledge sent from above,
You will know true contentment even when sad.

When you see too, that others also suffer,
When you can empathise with their pain,
When you can open your arms and welcome each other,
You will find fulfilment, a life free of blame.

Sara Church

As Calm As A Mill Pond

The slow undulations of a calm ocean
Like floating in a bath of calamine lotion
As water slowly slaps the boat
Softly on the wood floats
Dolphins pass smiling as usual
Yachts and tall ships for their perusal
Sardines swim in agitated silver spirals
Sharks fight among new arrivals
Suddenly the wind changes direction
Canvas moves with some discretion
Tall ships sail the same sea as power boats
Some sink and others float
A calm sea levels all sailing ships
As a captain sits and sips
Rum passed over chapped lips
Sea calm relaxes and frustrates
The racers whose teeth grate
But from an artistic view
Everything is fine and true.

Tim Sharman

Sowing Seeds

My thoughts
Are seeds,
Some take root,
Some do not,
Some I uproot,
And some I cultivate,
Like bonsai trees,
In the garden
Of my mind.

Trevor De Luca

GHOST GIRL

The beam of sunlight passes through my dust,
Like ashes of the dead that have already passed.
With no sense of who I am, I'm left amorphous,
Nothing more than flickers of light, as water on glass.
I glitter, and dance before your eyes.
Fragments of a soul that may leave you blind.
Can you feel my sadness hanging in the air?
A spirit in torment wondering if you know I am there.
I turn the air cold and you shiver in my arms,
Yet I whisper in comfort, please don't be alarmed.
Though I may feel so fragile as if I will shatter,
I need your embrace, please let me know that I matter.
Without your warmth, in the cold I'll remain;
No weapons with which to battle the pain.
And with one slight breeze the dust will disperse.
Bringing an untimely end to this shortened verse
But with time I am beginning to settle.
The flickers of dust in the afternoon's sun
Are starting to rest upon my tentative form.
A wavering existence is beginning to appear,
It's no longer the cold air that lets you know I am here.
As I walk on the sand I leave an imprint,
And if you follow in my path,
                              Then you'll know where I've been.
You can't look right through me as you used to do,
As my spectral form is beginning to take hue.
Though I remain like vapour in a lot of ways,
I'm working on making me whole some day.
Condensation doesn't always need to settle on pain;
The ethereal blue burns the hottest flame!

Caroline Roe

THIS ENGLAND

Oh what happened to this green and pleasant land?
I have the answer, but I do not understand,
In the fifties it was a glorious place,
Now I look around, I find it a disgrace,
With 'progress' that's been made in fifty years of time.
This sceptre isle should really be a place sublime.
We only used to have a 'Bobby' on the beat
Who kept law and order, and streets all clean and neat,
Rubbish, bottles, trash was put into the bin.
To throw it on the pavement was indeed a sin -
You did not fear to be out after dark;
Or catch the last bus home, and get mugged 'just for a lark.'
The driver stopped, if you put out your arm,
No chance of his passengers doing you harm.
'Postie' was a local chap, who knew all on his round,
He would bring your mail, and check you weren't lying on the ground,
He would take your letters to be posted to save your poor old legs,
A 'Romany' might call to sell you clothes pegs
Short arms and deep pockets to keep her takings in,
Her caravan her pride and joy, clean as a new pin,
Not like the 'Gipsy Lee' who presupposed today,
On any space available, and leaves rubbish on display,
Of bottles, tins and junk for the council to clear.
No wonder all our taxes are so very dear!
Graffiti splashed on many walls,
Churches, pubs and Civic Halls,
If today's 'Bobby' gave them what he should
He'd have broken the law, and lost his job for good.

Herdis Churchill

PLAYING WITH FIRE

There's a fascination with flames.
They lick almost lovingly and curl
Consuming all before them
And generating a warming glow.

A beautiful rainbow of colours
Flickering, draped in smoking twirls
Twisting this way and that
Upwards but then directionless.

You can try to smother this fire
Create a cloud of smoky confusion
But lift just one corner and air will flow
Breathing life into the flames once more.

Then, an explosion, all burning bright
And the fire is once more alive and licking
Giving light and warmth and cheer
To all those who are near.

But give it a poke and sparks may fly.
Beware, a furious surge of energy
Might just prove too much
And the smoke may choke you.

Fly just that bit too close
And your wings may be singed.
So, play by all means and enjoy
But beware the all-consuming fires of Heaven - or is it Hell?

Anne Rainbow

THE GHOST AT THROOP MILL

One late summer evening - very hot
I sat by the edge of the mill when,
A whisper came to my ear,
'What are you doing here?'
Leaping from the still weeds
Appeared a jolly dwarf lady.
Her face wrinkled and seedy pale,
'I'll tell you a secret of the poet'
She whispered in my ear.
'The owner still haunts the mill'
I stayed there till the full moon
And heard footsteps on the stairs
Sounding like a man running
With flour bags,
The dwarf lady whispered yet again,
'Will you greet him with a smile or tear?'
Then she disappeared like a deer.
I ran fast home and never
Ventured near again
That mill on my own!

Sammy Michael Davis

THE BEST MEDICINE

To ride a bike is healthy
Good for muscles, bum and tum
Teaches one to have good balance
And very cheap to run
Wear a protective helmet
As you pedal on the road
If you fall off the bicycle
It only should be bowed.

V A Coulson

BONFIRE NIGHT

Remember, remember, the fifth of November,
This verse, you know, is all rot,
For kids we adore, are making quite sure
That Guy Fawkes is never forgot.

They've been guying for weeks
And pennies they've sneaked,
A jumping Jack to acquire.
They let it off *'Pop!'*
Then skip and hop.
Of this fun they never will tire.

Remember, remember, the fifth of November,
Gunpowder, treason and plot.
Put fireworks away and kids on that day,
Have fun, say goodbye to the lot.

Joyce Walker

PLAYING THE PART

On a local television news bulletin, a report was transmitted
to show how an area police force was attempting to reduce
burglaries from elder peoples' homes.
This involved visiting an 'Over 60's Club' meeting and
staging possible scenarios to advise on methods of
preventing unwelcome visitors from gaining entry.
The cast of 'victims' and 'villains' was portrayed by
members of the local constabulary.
To conclude the item, an interview was held with the
officer-in-charge, who had organised the event, and the
following caption appeared at the bottom of the screen
to introduce him.
This read - *'Acting* Detective Inspector John Walsh.'

Brian M Wood

LUCKY

Sat unhappily tonight,
I have the smug defence
That 'happiness writes white',
And for only 54 pence

I can send away some lines,
To the editor in residence,
Who will recognise the signs of
Unadulterated genius.

I *could* have a couple of wah-wahs,
Dribbling in their bibs,
A semi-detached, a couple of Saabs,
A wife who digs me in the ribs

And nags from dawn till dinner time,
Spends my cash on shoes and shite,
Thinks getting drunk is a sinful crime
And that not one thing I do is right.

Stephen Taylor

PENNY

My little Penny the runt of the pack,
Completely contented and always laid back,
Do you know who she looks like?
Well she's like Spit the dog,
But she doesn't spit, she just gives you her love.
She is always untidy, her fur's never in place,
With her ginger eyebrows and a cute little face.
My little Penny as tatty as tatty can be,
But you know my little Penny is just a little like me.

Beryl Barlow

HALLOWE'EN

October thirty-first
A nightmare that's for sure
Kids come out in fancy dress
A banging on the door.

To say the words 'Trick or treat,'
Is the reason that they come
Another American import
That's a real pain in the bum.

That's the way I used to think
A grumpy, sad, old man
I really couldn't bear it
I was not its biggest fan.

But now that I am older
I've grown less sinister
This night is special to me
I'll get some visitors.

They come from all across the town
From every road and street
They only come to my house
'Cause they know I'll give them sweets.

For days like this I'm grateful
To kids just having fun
For this night I'm thankful
I've actually seen someone.

Neil Warren

THE CITY

The lamps of darkness gleam along the streets,
A route map of the city from the skies.
The avenues, plain urban in disguise
Of rural, quiet, self-contained retreats
Of solid citizens, lie dignified
Around the boundaries; while bedsit land,
Where students, junkies, beggars, hand-in-hand
Co-habit in unease and without pride
Infects the centre. Neighbours to these sorts,
The battlements of the department stores;
The offices of banks, solicitors;
The noisy bars; and on adjacent floors
To some of them, the doors - discreet - of whores.
Sleek cruisers hold the guardians of our laws;
Around the squares pedestrian echoes sound -
And taxi drivers, club and theatre bound,
Erratic and expensive pathways pound
To destinations halfway underground.
An incoherent mix, a state of mind,
The city is by man for man designed -
It is conglomerate, unkempt, unkind,
Exciting, lively, and to pity blind.

Maurice Coles

LETTING GO

Sorrow and joy, laughter and love,
Emotions so raw, simply echo above.
In life's endless hurry, worry and strife,
Of family, a mother, husband and wife.

Of parents suffering, each growing pain,
Children in love and will ever remain.
Growing, maturing, leaving the nest,
To pursue their feelings of teenage unrest.

You worry yet try to allow them to find out,
That learning experience, confidence and doubt.
All are part of the process coming of age,
You're weak, when you really need their courage.

So proud of the children, your flesh and blood,
The protection you've given and never could,
Ever stop them doing, what they want to do,
For now, they are wiser and stronger than you.

So don't worry and fret, let them find their own way,
For they see you as old, at the end of your day.
Be happy for them, put an end to your bother,
It's time to let go, and look after each other.

George Carrick

LAND OF MY DREAMS

I take the plunge into my mind's pool,
Departing from the real world, to a land of no rules.
My troubles now wander,
And I watch them disappear,
Reality has gone hazy,
My own world is now so clear.
I ride on my black horse,
And go far away,
The gust past my face,
Whispers my name.
The intense sensation,
That one of liberty,
Such a fine feeling,
To be free to be me.
Please don't wake me,
Come with me by all means,
And I'll welcome you,
To the land of my dreams.

Rosanna Anstice

The Lovely Young Lady In White

'Twas a lovely night,
When, at a disco,
I danced with a lovely young lady in white.
She wore a lovely long dress,
Made of lovely soft silk,
And just as white as milk.

She danced with such style and grace;
She had such a lovely face,
With a lovely personality;
So kind and sweet.
A better person,
I couldn't wish to meet.
Eventually, I had to leave,
To catch my train;
It was such a shame,
And I left her to dance into the night;
That lovely young lady in white.

Jason Pointing

UNTITLED

Words, letters lay lazily on the page.
Lifeless and dull.
Waiting patiently
For the day to come
When,
The covers of their bed
Are opened wide.

Words shiver in anticipation
    As eyes wander across their form.
The nouns, verbs, adjectives
    First mumble,
    Then raise up in chorus.

    As the reader
    Gazes upon the page.

New lines form
    Sentences, paragraphs and verse
All sing their song

    As the reader
    Gazes upon the page.

Till tiredness besets them
      Their energy spent.
The dance dies down.

    As the reader
    Lifts their gaze.

And the words,
      Again,
Sleep on in blissful slumber.
Waiting patiently,
For the next inquisitive mind
To hear their song.

Janet Ayerman

THOUGHTS FOR SOLITUDE:
FROM GRANNY EILEEN, WITH LOVE

You say you are your own man,
A laid back self-sufficient fellow;
That you've learned all you can:
No more a-stripling callow.

But I would challenge you:
What are your inmost resources?
'I'm bored - what can I do?'
Without outside exciting forces.

Close your eyes, not just to sleep.
Where lie your goals? What is your bent?
Is it wise? Look inward deep
'My daddy doles; they're heaven-sent.'

Must others shape your lot?
Or does life involve input, output?
Keep adding to assets you've got.
Stoke up the fires, sweep up the soot.

Deduct the mindless monitor's game,
Trash the futile skateboard.
What remains? You look the same
But brain and body are ignored.

Thoughts and muscles need honing
And ideals, not hair, role models.
It's no use your groaning
Too much shelter just coddles.

When you rise each day, look outward.
Embark upon a learning curve.
Say silently, 'I'm not an isle of others rid
But part of many whom I must serve.'

Eileen Ellis-Whitfield

MY HALLOWE'EN

Silently they came to my door,
A witch, ghost, skeleton and goblin, just four
With broom, lantern, a wand for spells,
'We have come to haunt you,' they yell.
The witch, with wand in hand, pointed at me,
Her face a horrid luminous green,
She was the best I've ever seen.
Skeleton with white, glistening bones,
Chattering teeth, said, 'I wished I'd stayed at home.'
Goblin, perfect in every way,
Didn't have much to say.
It was the ghost that intrigued me.
As smoke from around its knees
Rose eerily to the sky.
Most effective I thought, with a sigh.
Then a face appeared from around its back
That was a good one, I laughed.
I think now, you had better come in
And have your treat to begin.
For I don't want to be like you as well.
So here you are, a pound apiece
And a sandwich of bread and cheese.
Then wash it down with this witches brew.
Thank you for this night of horror,
For I know it won't happen tomorrow.

Robert Gray Sill

CHRISTMAS SHOPPING

Busy shoppers in the street
Where down in Nottingham
They will meet
Other people every day
Busy shopping for Christmas Day.

It is hustle and bustle
With bargains galore
And no matter what you spend
You always need more.

There are presents for the children
Mums and dads
Not forgetting your friends
So take lots of wads.

Then there's food to buy
Decorations and all
How we love Christmas
We are having a ball.

It is once a year
So go round the bend
Whiz round the stores
And spend and spend.

Eddie Jepson

ENGLISH COMMANDMENTS

Thou shall not smoke fags in public places at will,
I've suffered passive smoking for almost eighty years up until,
Yet they have not knackered my lungs so far,
I wonder if they are covering up the root cause of this phenomena.

Thou shall not hunt foxes with thy dog on a horse,
Well I wouldn't dream of doing such a thing of course,
My dog can't ride a horse and foxes have never done me any harm,
But I know I'd think differently if I were running a farm.

Thou shall love thy ethnic neighbour like a brotherly man,
Well here again, I don't know if I really can,
If he cannot adapt to blending to life here and our law,
Or learn to understand and work within the HASAW Act 1974.

Thou shall not covet thy neighbours bit of stuff,
Not even after a hot curry, known to make some like a bit of rough,
Only in cities of culture are conditions set apart,
Where a man can visit a brothel and hire himself a tart.

Thou shall not kill, except of course in the event of war,
Like the government have mistakenly sent you before,
Then only when situation code word *wisdom* comes to pass,
Translated meaning, Weapons Intelligence Suspect - Destruct On Mass.

Young MP's bulldozing laws through, by hook or by crook,
Just to gain fame, and get their names in the statute book,
Not one of them mentioning laws affecting all constituents,
Such as modern housing for millions at affordable rents.

I cannot recall even one of them giving a mention,
To the restoration of the workers' contributory pension,
Only prattle about catching the criminals and sending them to jail,
Where we know that leniency and rehabilitation, will again fail.

Jack Edwards

BETWEEN

Chestnuts on a bonfire, hear them pop and crackle
Apple pie, what wrapped in foil lies within?
A coin for wealth? A ring for marriage? Or maybe a stick for poverty?
The flames flicker against the wintry night's sky
Shadows leap as we crowd in, sharing in the fire's welcome heat.
A time for family and friendship
A time for fun as our serious faces we cast aside.
Something about that fire that pulls us closer
Draws us nearer, breaks down barriers.
Between the old and the new
Between this world and the next.
A time before, an age long ago
Bring the flocks in from the hills
The final harvest of the year.
Leave a meal out for the dead
Our loved ones now to be welcomed back.
Snuff the fire from the hearth
To be relit from the Druid's flame.
Don't be tricked by the fairies
On this day between the years.
Between the now and the then
Between the lies and the truth
On the morning after, all that is left of the fire is charred remains
Coals that cannot be relit.
Beneath the scorched soil though
So many layers
That if we were to choose to peel back it would bring us closer.
Between the generations
Between the lost and the found
Between the modern and the ancient
Under the veil of Hallowe'en, in the flicker of those dancing flames
I hope you find a connection, something more than tricks and treats.

Simon Wright

LAITING WITCHES

Not so very long ago in ancient Lancasheer,
Folku'd be laiting witches, at this time of year.
Old Moll would lead the way, candle in her hand
Along the lanes and roads all about the land.
The children brought their candles, coming at a run,
Following behind her, eager, every one
To find the witches out, wherever they were hid.
Even if they never knew what 'twas the witches did.
When the candle flames grew small, or if they all went out,
Then everybody knew that a witch was hereabout.
But what were they supposed to do, whenever one was found?
Well, nobody ever said, so, not making any sound,
Went creeping home to safety and made a note of place,
Where they knew a witch was hiding but, they never saw her face.

Betty Norton

GENOCIDE

There is no such terror as, like the terror of war
The whine of bullets, the screaming of shells
The victims hugging the ground for dear life
The screams of the wounded and the dying
Bodies sprawled over the blood-drenched soil
Nation against nation, dying for their beliefs
Genocide, that is the name of the game, the
True horror of war is, that it is always the
Innocent who have to pay the price, but
Who will stop it, no one can, one war stops
Another begins, enabling some evil people
To grow rich on blood-stained money, that
Is the modern way of life, God help us all.

Guthrie

RACE AWARE

Pick two numbers from one to six
And go and lay your bets,
But when the race is over
Let you not forget

Through the roar of the crowd
The dust in the air
They'll be chasing all out
For the mechanical hare!

Yes, greyhounds are graceful
                    with muscles of steel
But when finished at four
                    they get a raw deal.
A sofa and fire are what they desire
With lots of love and attention
                    when they retire.

A L Wingate

THE CIGARETTE CARD COLLECTOR

He collected and loved them
They were his pride and joy
He collected with pleasure
Since he was a boy

He stored them in safety
And when he had two
He swapped one for another
On a subject quite new

He cherished and kept them
In an old Golden Flake tin
And now his descendants
Have thrown them all in the bin

Clive Atkins

HALLOWE'EN DOWN HORROR STREET

It's the night where out comes,
The witches,
The ghosts,
The monsters.

With a switch of doorbell
And the presents of sweets
And the attack of eggs,
There is a flow of colour.

There is a distant yell
Of 'Trick or treat'
And the jingle of money.
That's the feel of one night.

The person standing at the door,
Is aware, knowing that behind the opaque door,
Is not small children, but a gang,
Out to collect.

Amy Herbert (14)

University Ceremonials

It all seems quite ridiculous,
So pompous and antique.
A throw back to the old times,
Tradition, so to speak.
The hierarchy trundle in
And sit up on the stage.
Graduates sit and ponder,
Will this give me a wage?
One by one, they tip their lids
And bow and dip to betters.
They take their due and pass along,
And hear the men of letters.
Row on row they process through,
Clutching paper hopes and dreams,
Ending one phase, new to come,
A promise, so it seems.
Am I a cynic? Perhaps a bit,
But then I hear my name.
I tip my lid and take my due
And reverently do the same.

Patricia Adele Draper

THINKING OF YOU

I think of you constantly but some places bring thoughts of you even closer, memories of happy times spent together or just associations

Bank, Bayswater, Brick Lane, Blackfriars, Earl's Court, Embankment, Fleet Street, Leicester Square, Liverpool Street, Oxford Street, Queensway, Strand, Victoria, Whiteleys, Wood Street, Starbucks, Kenya, the list goes on

However, the closest I get to you in your absence is when I see, hear or read about Notting Hill, on tubes, buses, maps, television or in books and newspapers. My heart jumps every time I hear those two words

But there is one place where I have very strange feelings, although we have never been there together. When I am sitting in Sloane Square I think about you, wishing you were with me, feeling both close to and far away from you at the same time.

I spend a lot of time in London because I feel closer to you there, even though we are apart. But wherever I find myself, I am thinking of you all the time . . .

Nash

To A Teddy

I cleared my drawers in a hurry
Time waits for no one - in a flurry of books, old manuscripts of rhyme
I must do more with time.

And the deadline it was nearing
With heavy hands, unsubtle clearing left my prize possessions in a heap
I have targets to keep.

There's no time to be limp-wristed
All out and into boxes listed into categories of thing;
Have I got everything?

Teddy! Silent there on my table
In you go - squeeze you, no - unable to fit you down the side!
I'll carry you outside.

Why? In God's name, why worry?
It's scraps of cloth but sod the hurry, there's more to it than just a bear
It's a real creature there.

I can't squash my poor old teddy
He sat with me till I was ready to leave my home and journey
                                                on the road

And then safely stowed.

Fraser Hicks

THE WARTIME FORK?

The fork I use in the garden,
Its handle: mortised, tenoned,
Pinned and worn;
Has 'unity' written on its shaft.
This grape with flattened prongs,
Must have been used by many a hand.
From one of a few houses, it could have come,
Though, it seems to have been around
Since perhaps the second one;
Was it Hurdles, maybe Giles?
Then again, it could have been -
'Oh, I don't know!'
But I'm sure it was old even then,
Maybe of wartime use, hence 'unity'
When grown-ups (I was a baby then);
Dug for victory and of course to eat,
Shielding us mentally from possible defeat.

John L Wigley

CHEEKY BIRD

One day a young baby starling,
Fell out of its nest in my garden,
It hopped on my knee
Saying, 'Oh, silly me!
If I scared you, I do beg your pardon.'

J Higgs

A SPELL IN HOSPITAL

A darkened ward at 2.00am,
Awake with seven snoring men,
When an old chap, in the corner bed
Sat bolt upright and quite clearly said,
'I now declare this meeting open!'
Then, with the silence truly broken,
'You may have heard, I'm sad to say,
That as Chairman, I resign today,
But who will fill my shoes you ask?
For it will be no easy task,
To lift this business from decline,
The responsibility was mine.'

With no reply from any fellow
Frustrated he began to bellow,
'Now come on chaps, some input please,
This company is on its knees!
Your attitude I find absurd,
Will no one here put in a word?'
An air of silence all around,
And still no answer to be found,
He shouted, 'Well, if that's the case,
I think this Board's a damned disgrace!'
Then wrapped up in his dressing gown,
He quite serenely lay back down.

Mark L Moulds

TERRORISM

Right from the start of time and beyond,
Terrorists have tried to seek some bond,
Often pitting rebel forces, bitterly opposed,
With loss of life beyond those involved.

Kingdoms and states have been laid waste,
Brutal regimes led to many dead.
In haste, poverty was the rule of everyday's fate
Every rescue programme being far too late.

Apart from wars and the results therein,
Terror and riots would not be far in gain,
Slowly communism began to lose its way,
In its place democracy had its day.

Then came the dreaded Sept 11th,
Sombre day, no sign or clue gave these events away.
Along with these horrific eventualities,
Came more and sinister world tragedies.

Our world from being orthodox and calm,
Became in that short time one of storm,
Life styles normally so complete,
Became scary in terms of defeat.

Holidays and ways of life so normal
Turned overnight just abnormal,
Hopes that life could get straight,
Would surely be so very great.

B Burkitt

A DARKER SHADE OF LIGHT

(Dedicated to S J Seiglow)

I do not look at you with eyes of a darker shade of light
Heart and mind held captive by an hourglass
Although with time, you have changed
Yet I still do not look at you
With eyes of a darker shade of light.

No longer young, I freely admit,
But I cannot look at you
With eyes of a darker shade of light.
When night comes and before me, naked you stand
The scars of time are never in my sight.

Then in the stillness, lying next to me
I only see that maiden of my youth
And if in old age, the Lord should dim my sight
He is only making sure
I can never look at you with eyes of a darker shade of light.

D G Seiglow

SOMETHING TO BELIEVE

You think this isn't me, well that's so sweet and I'm so sorry.
Of all absurdities, this is the worst,
you are unfortunate, and I don't want you to think
I need you to be part of my dreams
(dreams are soft mumblings recited by non-believers.)
Comparison denies us the ability to believe in ourselves.
It is not enough for others to fail, we must watch them
admire us for our compassion towards them,
and then we convince ourselves that we are the deserving.
Oh, denial is a glorious thing
it makes us reach inside ourselves and see only just enough.

Lucy Bradford

ANGLAIS FRAPPÉ (OR BACK TO SYNTAX)

I bought a new designer shirt
And sat it at a table
With paper, pen and drawing board
To see if it was able.
I left it for an hour or two,
My hopes were high and many,
When I returned were there designs?
Indeed there were not any!

My friends all thought one Christmas time
That they'd do me a favour
When gleefully they gave to me
The latest batt'ry shaver.
'Oh thank you very much,' I said
(To give offence I'm wary)
'Whatever can I use it for?
My batteries aren't hairy!'

'Be sure,' they said, 'to eat such food -
As that is good and healthy.'
'Indeed I do. Oh yes!' I cried
'Although I am not wealthy.
For rotten food that is diseased,
May terminate my living,
But healthy food may better taste
And even be health giving!'

G A Baker

A Poet's Gift

What is this art of poetry
Tell - is it something to endure?
Ideas and words that need spreading
Like medication as a cure.

Is poetry a welcome flair
Is it something to share about?
The thoughts inside our minds to grow
Like flowers as they open out.

And this poetry, expanding
Onto paper and into print
Is it always worth the anguish
Or is life seen thru' rosy tint?

The poet's eye is reflective
Notions like sounds inside their heads
Emotions felt, without touching
And moving forward on life's treads.

The words, they have great importance
As they spill out onto the page,
Working silently and alone
Expressing love, insight or rage.

But this work is almost complete
The final phrases have been writ
Time taken - willingly given
It's a poem: a poet's gift.

Doreen Fillary

MY LOST LOVE

Last year, a bad year
Every day, badness came
Constantly fighting, a mighty fight
Overwhelming weakness, stress had no rest

Loving encouragement, strength enduring
We couldn't give, only bitterness
Cold hearts developed, hope diminished
Our association finished, the last day

Alone, entering the new year, missing my children dearly
For you I pray, pray in hope one day
Bearing every second, the dagger sinks deep
Without my children, life has no meaning

A loving, happy home would have made the difference
Goodbye for now, my love
Death's door has come knocking
A new era has begun

Innocent children being hurt; my children
One day your eyes will see that
My heart bleeds until that day comes
Open your eyes my love, my lost love.

George Petrie

WHY?

A worm was wriggling along the ground
Which raised a question I thought quite profound:
Why doesn't it wear its underside out
Or has it protection we don't know about?

Who leads the flock and chooses the way
When birds fly in formation - do they all have a say?
What happens to him if his choice is not right
And there's only sea with no land in sight?

And when the tide rushes off, away from the shore
Eager for mischief and mayhem galore
Where does it go to tease or to pound
And who gives the signal which turns it around?

How do bulbs in the ground know when to come through
Down there in the dark without compass or clue?
And how about moles who come up to the light
From their tunnels to feed when the time is just right?

So many mysteries left to resolve
While Nature continues its plans to evolve
How many years needed to absorb all that's said?
Well I'd better get started - there's no time for bed!

Betty Nevell

REVELATION

In Revelation's symbology
It's 666 that holds the key
These numbers written, plain as day
That show us how we've lost our way

These numbers are the reason for
The starving nation's global wars
Why man's deceptions justify
Manipulations, frauds and lies
Brother to brother, father to son
Friend to neighbour, everyone

We want, we need, we lust with greed
We lie, we cheat, we all compete
Our history has been this way
For our survival, day to day
Enough to eat so we might live
But we have lost the will to give

This talk of Armageddon
The cloven beast, the Devil's son
But it is plain if we would see
That numbers really are the beast
It's those that drive the global greed
And they depend on those in need

This system built in ancient times
Creates the laws, defines the crimes
But what's been lost in history
Is man and his humanity
We fear for what might end this world
Meteor showers, climatic ruin
But we don't need these things to come
If we continue as we have done

We place our needs above our souls
Material aims, not spiritual goals
So little do we understand
About the meaning of a man

And if there is a truth to find
Material greed has made us blind
Until we take the time to look
Instead of trusting in the books

In books we can manipulate
Define the truth to suit the state
If truth exists it's universal
Not only based around this world
It's only truth which can make us whole
And that my friend lies in the soul.

Robert Wallace

LIKE A FOLLY

The wasteland you see in him
A charcoal tree
Black and yield in the saccharine wilderness
Pain eternal
Appear like cracks to the pale moon
The murky secrets haunted
In the wake
Love loses bearing, passionless the purple wind
The strangled flower, running through your head
In the token sunrise
Flies gather round black angels
In a folly of numb pain
You can be my mentor in my borrowed coat.

Colin Beck

THE STREET SCENE

Crime is on the rise, truly it brings tears to my eyes
everyday, someone is dying from senseless violence,
makes you wonder, are we really trying?

Makes no sense to me how the guilty can maim and kill
the innocent and just get away Scott free. At the same
token, I appreciate the fact we have law enforcement.

You can't live in this world without it, no matter where
we go, there will always be crime. I don't know any place
where it doesn't exist. It has become part of daily
living, yet we must bear in mind and never forget all
those brave men and women who put their lives on the line
every day to assure our safety, this is what they are giving.

Lorraine Jackson

CYMRU

To be born Welsh is to be born with song in blood and bone
With hireath in the heart that esteems horizon-home
From white-headed winter Snowden down to Teifi's waterfalls
The lure of the Red Dragon whose younglings 'ere recall
A childhood blessed with tolerance and laced with laughter sweet.
Where tears were brief and transient and forgiveness quick to greet.
Full Gentiles dwell in Cymru as mellifluous as their speech
Yet resolute their tenets and in conflict stern to beat.
Comb the ragged fleeces of the rugged mountain sheep
And nuzzle sturdy ponies whose heathered grazing keep
The hills, like new-mown lawns that top the coal and rock
Which fuelled the fires of London and built the Cardiff dock
However far they travel, the truth at end of days
Is that folk magnet homewards to spend life's waning phase.

Sarah Blackmore

EARTH AND I

We breathe together,
this Earth and I . . .
White man mines our heart
pollutes our soul,
tears our hair,
pierces our skin,
feeds us with poison,
clouds our eyes,
suffocates us until we choke,
covers us with concrete,
binds us in buildings,
bruises us where they walk,
crawling across our skin.

They taint our tears
until life dries up.
And there is no place for shelter,
nothing to eat
nothing to love with.

Taking, taking, taking . . .

Then you'll leave.
And we'll lie bruised,
naked,
cold
in the dark.

We bleed together
this Earth and I . . .

Such arrogance to think
that I could ever hurt as much as our
Mother Earth . . .
I am flogged by few.
She is mutilated by millions.

Tracey Levy

YESTERDAY'S VALLEY

Spring again is gone, and summer, was he my friend?
Autumn now her warning sends with tears,
as gorse clings to the weeping hill and the
willow bends, deep.

The kestrel, high, fat with summer's glow
knowing and yet fatter, he must go
to stand the winter's blow and spies
with eagle-eye, his dinner down below,
now another small tear will rise.

Down the valley of the Shibe in September weather,
As valleys go, here green grows the grass,
no reluctance here.
And there, beneath the lowest bow, a stream,
a thousand years has flowed,
to avert the Calder's fears.

I have bought the Lord's wares from His basket
of the world, paying with my conscience
and my breath.

Make your way down the Dean and leave no stone
unturned, until you reach the valley's bed.
Where oak and beech and other stately kings
with purpose, fill the day. To guide and shelter
you and with beauty pave your way.

This heavenly hollow in our midst,
this street of nature's charms, this unspoilt babe,
forever, has nestled in his arms.

Much greener grows the grass, 'tis said,
but the grass of the valley of the Shibe
is an inheritance, greener yet.

There are rocky paths here, and muddy trails
for non who are too wide.
But not a path in all this valley, that endeavour
cannot stride . . .

(Shibe) archaic for Shibden

Eric Langford

MOONLIGHT

I sat at my table and wrote,
on paper glowing by candlelight.
I sat and stared at the snow outside
my thoughts quivered like unsure candlelight.

I stood with the kettle as it boiled,
steam shimmered by candlelight.
I sat back at the table, hot drink down,
observing a cup of refracted candlelight.

I watched the yellowed walls as they danced,
in the shadows furnished from candlelight.
I took my scarf and coat and viewed from my door
the snow outside as I was backlit by candlelight.

I ventured outside in the chill of midwinter,
bereft from the warmth of candlelight.
The once expanse of green trees and field
were white with snow gleaming from the sense of moonlight.

Alex Harford

CHOCOLAT

Once held in high regard,
a Gilded God, high street bound,
you beckon in sultry tones,
sugar-sweet, black as bitter night.

Magnetising, you murmur
a promise of paradise, an explosion,
expedient to the senses, luxuriating
in the longed for, yet limited moment,
stolen in secrecy, alone in a side street,
side-stepping from the babble of voices
for one sweet release.

Afterwards, sated of desire,
Guilt plays upon the shore of your departing.
Why?
An answer that only the smile of Mona Lisa
can tell of; until the next time.

Alison Jones

WATCHING

On night watching,
So I am host
Blokes asleep
In their trench
Fought quite hard
We jolly well did
Next battle down
Or so they say
Leave one awake
Others have kip

Michael D Bedford

THINKING OF YOU

Wild life is it all
The sun shines a ray
Time is it really all
OK?
Tune my head in
Judge day by day
I'm just thinking all
I can say

If you see a silent sigh
And you ask the question, 'Why?'
If you see a shooting star
Then I'm thinking of you
And if a line strays from a keen
And a curve turns to a coil
And you feel the falling rain
Then I'm thinking of you

A kestrel flew
Beside my car
And for ten minutes
It was all OK.
Cold and freezing
Sat in a park
Trees, ice and moon
And it's OK.

If you see a silent sigh
And you ask the question, 'Why?'
If you see a shooting star
Then I'm thinking of you
And if a line strays from a keen
And a curve turns to a coil
And you feel the falling rain
Then I'm thinking of you.

Jonny Loader

THE UNIVERSITY OF LIFE

No wonder,
It's good to go to university,
It's a springboard to the future,
The future of the world

Nothing can beat education,
Education is the ultimate,
If you can achieve this much,
You're ready for the world

You'll be able to experiment,
Make a go of things,
But, above all,
Gain a place in the world,
For all it's worth

The University of Life,
It's a springboard to the future,
Nothing can beat education,
Education is the ultimate.

No wonder,
You're unique,
In the world of education.
It'll hold you in good stead.

John Floyd

BLESSINGS

I have the sun to shine by day,
To keep me warm and light my way.

And when in bed at night I sleep,
The moon and stars their watch to keep.

I have the showers and summer breeze
The garden crops and leafy trees.

A garden for my leisure hours
In country lanes and wayside flowers.

Amazing creatures, small and great;
Far too many to contemplate.

Changing seasons guaranteed,
Food to satisfy my need.

Loving friends their help to give
A comfy home in which to live.

God's creation all around
Wonders, blessings, that abound.

Every day my thanks I give
For the gifts that I receive.

Though a sinner self-confessed
With what wonders I am blessed.

Janet Cavill

EPIPHANY

It held certainty, but powerless
On a drifting windswept shore:
Dotted with pewter stones
And gnarled forked branches,
The past catching the present
In a faint red-haired outline
Of a long lost love.

We are tried and tested
In these lapping waves of thought
Invested with some invisible
Higher authority;
Waiting for our time to reach culmination.
Waiting for our due heritage.
Waiting for our endless epiphany
To come to its conclusion.

We took turns
Opening each other's heart and mind;
Then fast-tracked
To some subtle bed lair
After toasting our common ancestor:
Bloodline symmetries
Of flesh and bone.
This is for the times
We met and photographed
The wind in our hair,
Like distant lovers
Stroking the same soft skin
Of hidden desire;
Now buried in damp earth
To remind us all
Of our fleeting life
And to reach our spirit home:

Surrounded by dreams
Wrapped in a cradle
Of returned kisses
In no-man's-land.

Peter Corbett

THE POWER AND BEAUTY IN YOUR EYES

(Dedicated to Augustina Ifeoma Uwaoma)

Your heavy-lidded bright
Iridescent eyes gleam as
The blues and greens and golds
That give richness
And warmth to the day.
They glitter with a layer of
Bright shining crystals
They catch the morning light
Sending purple lasers all through
The oceans of royal blue spread.
They cause moonlight to shimmer
On the sea
So that the plankton are disturbed
And when they are disturbed
They look so beautiful on sea surface
Shining like crystals.
The lashes in your eyes
As beautiful and well arranged
As a feather-like collection of
Small crystals in which snow falls.

Martins Ayere Edo

RICHER FIELDS?

The grass seems always greener,
In the place where it's not
When you decide to walk away -
The past is soon forgot.

To richer fields you think you'll head
And when you reach the horizon
You start to dread.

For those greener fields have disappeared,
Your past forgotten?
The future nears.

So decide you must
Before it's too late
Will your past take you back -
Or is the future to be great?

Laura O'Rourke

SHADOW BOXING

When I'm with you
I try.

Without you
Silence again.

Pain after pain.

A Lee Firth

LIVES BEFORE

To hold each other in our arms,
so loving and tight,
fills us both,
with pure delight.

Our lives before,
were unkind and unjust,
but now being together,
is a definite must.

Before we fought,
with pain and emotion,
now what we have,
is love, happiness and devotion.

Being in love with you,
is sheer wonder and bliss,
not being near you,
is something I miss.

Peter Bayliss

THE NIGHT

The light is fading from the sky
To the sun we'll soon have to say goodbye
The moon will then show its face
The sun we'll see no trace
The night is sometimes very eerie
But not always noticeable when you're weary
The stars are sometimes very bright
Lovely to lie and watch at night
The night gives you different feelings
While watching shapes move across the ceilings
But then it's time to close those eyes
And to say goodnight until the sunrise.

B Crouzieres

WARMTH TO THOSE IN THE COLD

Many are the ones who fought
Cold and distraught
Emblems go forth
Banners for joy
To see the end
Of the rules they bend
Will sanity 'will do' part
And from the heart
It was a problem
From the very start
For honour we shall not part
And wherever you lay your hat
That's my best part
For the world always charts
The best of me and yes, you
Always we pay our dues
And like knights duel
Through and through
Grit and gruel
No matter how cruel.

Hardeep Singh Leader

A GIRL OF THE RIVER

A girl of the river,
he married her.
Took her back to his place.
They lived there.
He said everything would be all right.

They lived in a stone-brick cottage.
He was a native of these parts.
He used to cockfight.
She like to darn and knit.
They had four kids,
three girls, one boy,
born one winter after another.

She was a girl of the river.
Sometimes he hit her,
but never that hard.
Just to mind her
of what was right from wrong, he said.
He was always right.
She was just a simple thing.
One day she killed him.

Andy Botterill

THE SKY

The sky is fickle like the sea
Ever changing, ever free
Morning comes, dark curtain drawn outside
To show pale colour of dawn.
A slow transition comes about
Pinks and greens and blues appear
To herald the sun, slowly climbing
To banish moon and midnight clear.
As day begins, pale colours give way
To sky of blue
The sun, well up, lends its colour and hue
Fluffy white clouds dot the expanse
As of cotton wool they do a puffball dance.
A single plane soars on its way
Turning to silver in glinting sun
Children gather in the park to play
With watchful parent looking on.
The rainbow mantle of the sky
Enfolds the world till night is nigh.

Edna Freeland

DON'T

Don't leave me
Stay within the blood that adores you:
Singing your hot praises -
Without either I am less.

There are lakes within me and a thousand deserts
All merged as a sea of dry mouthings.
You leave me tracks -
And I tread lightly; not to disturb.

Gary T Pollard

EAST TO WEST

How did you find yourself here my girl?
    At five o'clock in the morning
        And you in white satin selling yourself

Whilst the traffic lights spill their colours
    Across the shiny wet tarmac. Once
        I'm sure you lived on a farm,

Loved the sting of the wind, the light in the grass
    And flung your bare arms around a dog's furry neck.
        Ah, I know. You developed while the land

Went sere and your parents dried out
    Before your eyes like grapes left to the sun.
        Then a gold-chained man drove up in a BMW

With what seemed like an exciting idea.

Paul Ellarby

SAYING THE PINK ROSARY

A man I didn't know offered me
a pink rosary while we were waiting
outside the confessional at the Shrine.
Now I'm not a rosary man
and pink was never my colour.

Cheap and tacky, out of a holy cracker,
but he offered it as though it were
a special treasure that would
keep me safe and guard me
on the stormy journey through life.

So I took it from him in that spirit
and it was.

Michael Cunningham

CLEANING

so small that you unwittingly fill the room
compressing molecules until they resemble twilight,
and as you tidy away dinner plates and cutlery
in the shapes of tears

it is me that recognises your pain, your anger/frustration
it is me that sees you hid behind positrons
weeping on neutrons
standing on top of solar systems, reaching out to me

you brush the dust of madness under the carpet
as i dirty the walls with the mud of jealousy
then glue together the fragile pieces of friendship

as we creep in the hallways of deceit
straightening the picture frames of lust
we realise that everything is tidy except our hearts

Stephen Emmerson

HALF-SHUT

So I'm sitting here
Losing focus with the light
Waiting.
The fact that my eyes are half-shut will not deter me
For as long as it takes, I'll still be here
Expectant.
Reflecting on all those who have gone before me
And all who will pass after me
In your humble, distinguished life.
And the purest thing I can tell you at this very moment is this:
I would stay up for all the nights of my life
If only the last one was with you.

Elizabeth Toop

INTAKE OF '63 AND ME

(Aged 11 then)

Christopher B . . . 'Barney', unashamedly me
and good pal 'Oscar', Andrew C;
Faye C . . . heartthrob of any real man, including me, very loveable,
Ian C . . . now a barrister, so Colesy you keep 'em out of trouble;
Stephen D . . . was 'Bill', dad's profession was a bill poster,
Linda G . . . had such a spotty crush on her!
Brian H . . . got the 'Hicky',
Jacqueline H . . . think she rode horses, our Jackie
Anita J . . . 'Swiss Miss', think it was something to do with the boots
Andrew M . . . was 'Rupert', something to do with the puppet in a box
and his curly long hair right from the roots!
Susan M . . . 'Mazz', was ginger and lovely,
Jane M . . . 'Parsley', blonde lioness of Magic Roundabout fame
on the BBC!
Joanne M . . . was very sophisticated and
'Oggy' . . . 'Colin O' such a brainy Geordie lad, now
a surgeon, steady hand
and Patricia H . . . 'Hawkeye', don't be put off by her nickname,
she was lovely again,
Andrew P . . . 'Pop', this one,
Gail R . . . slim, brunette, lovely doll,
Jane S . . . cuddly, lovely and naughty with it,
Darryl S . . . 'Daz', after the popular washing powder
at the time,
Phil S . . . big in the police, thin blue line
Peter W . . . 'Wad', for loading a gun,
Mark W . . . another 'Wad' now studies the Sun!
Robert W . . . 'Wiggy', sort of fitted his name and his hairstyle,
Jane W . . . lovely, tall, fresh complexion, long legs too,
knew her quite a while!
Stuart W . . . 'Woody', always had a smile!
Sorry if your name's not been mentioned but maybe you didn't come
to the reunion.
Will miss you lots anyway.

Chrisbarnespoet

THE TRUTH WILL OUT

Your eyes reveal the truth, do not lie
    I am investigating those sorrows that you must not deny
Unable to be true this is the pathway that led
    To others who invaded; where, oh where, was I to tread?
You appear to seek forgiveness and its contents to refrain
    Causing many heartaches and of mine the bitterest of pain
You being a committed schemer I know I shall never win
    As soon as you have finished with this affair, you will
                                    commence over again.

I thought I really cared for you, but now I doubt my mind
    You are so unreliable and love, absolutely blind
How could you appreciate others, leaving me
    Being requested of love as now I wander free
Refusing to be tied down and committed to only one
    Apparently you have a choice and a great deal more fun
So many are your followers as you parade and flirt
    Considered an entertainer, you are desirous of your work

True love, you do not know the meaning
    As to your fickle heart you may never adapt
Meandering as you will, there can be no prospects
    And all you come in contact with, will laugh back
This truth will out and its sorrow
    Maybe to pursue on some unkindly track
None will ever come to appreciate your meaning
    Flitting the while as you briefly look back.

R D Hiscoke

CAN YOU MISS SOMEONE TOO MUCH?

My inspiration comes from extremes of emotions
But extremely dead doesn't seem to count
Since I lost you, I've lost my light
All I feel is this ghostly torment

Every break-up song and love song
Reminds me (as if I'd forgotten about you), again
Yet I don't connect with them the way I used to
Even nature's telling me, it's in frosty, whipping winds and
                              perennial, ripping rains.

My friends don't understand it, you know
They think I'm just mad. Guess they've never felt it so true
                              and pure and strong
Maybe it would have been better if we'd argued
Shouted and screamed and all blown up.
At least it would have been over, I wouldn't feel this for so long.

People can die of broken hearts, right?
OAPs I mean, all their lives together, then having to . . .
Bury half of themselves, saying the long goodnight
Or is it all just coincidental, and due to only old age?

How many months has it been now?
Sick as it is, I'd rather not know if you're even still alive
Thinking of you with someone else fills me with something
                              beyond sorrow
Guess I was in too deep. Yet I'm still sinking deeper and lower.
                              Do I need to dive?

Anya Lees

AN INSTINCTIVE LIFE

An instinctive life, is there any such thing
Or are we not, rather, plotting and scheming,
Plans for the future, managing debt.
Practical matters dictate and yet
How much of this planning derives from dreaming,
Seeing the autumn blooms in spring?

Always anticipating something better,
Some new conception, a possible cure.
Even our rational bets are uncertain,
Old enthusiasms gone for a burton,
Still we await the unexpected letter,
A win on the lottery today for sure.

What matter the glad surprise is late?
My instinct is to sit and wait.

Geoff Tomlinson

NO TIME

It is time
Wait! Wait!
It will come
Time will have my moment
And pass -
Reflected in the eye of a petrified fly
Still -
On the bark,
Shed in the tangled growth
Brushing over all -
Never to go
Never to stay
Never to come back again

E C Mulvaney

I Should Die

I wanted to melt before you, sharpened your dagger;
Before that lust for blood I wanted so sublime,
And before that I wanted to go underground.

But you have to have the seatbelt in your car,
Put up a pillar or a signpost to support your roof,
You must have the fire cylinder.

Keep on your side,
Don't drive under liquor influence,
Look for the signposts.
Yes, look out for pedestrians,
And don't speak on your mobile when spinning.

Not to say that I'm afraid of death;
'Tis my son who must learn,
'Tis my daughter who's in need of clothing.
'Tis my wife that needs a shoulder to lean on.
Otherwise I want to die,
Not only die but be forgotten.

Koa

Make It

Our aims in life are all the same, to work hard and to gain,
To navigate, negotiate, participate and strain.
Aiming for that mountain top that seems away on high,
Forgetting now that in the end we are all going to die.
Get up early, beat the rush, hurry on your way,
In the end for me there will be an even bigger pay.

Paul Kangley

ON THE SIDELINES

Sitting on the sidelines.
Just waiting - to be with you.
Hoping for the sweet scent of you,
wishing for emotions - to be proven true.

Sitting on the sidelines,
always there - just to be with you.
Wishing for the scent and sight,
of someone, I love so true.

Sitting on the sidelines,
hoping a prayer - will be answered.
As I sit stewing and ponder,
my situation in life,
            my desire of you.

Gary J Finlay

I LOVE YOU

I   love you

L ove is you and I
O thers can't see
V irtually what you mean to me
E ach of us has loved before but

Y ou are the one, the
O ne I need, we have a
U nique kind of love.

Kayleigh Brandon

WHAT REMAINS

You're a ghost
I saw you before
Hollow inside, nothing more
Dust on a shelf
Dark beneath the waves
I've killed you once
I'll kill you again
Only this time I won't be in pain
You will be simple
Plain
Look back
Remember my name
I will always be here
Always be the same
You won't change this body
For only this shell remains.

Bryony Freeman

UNTITLED

I'll love the gold
If of gold, you're dressed yourself
Gold around your hair,
Gold around your hips,
Gold on your fingers,
. . . Gold on you,
Pure iced metal.

Annamaria Pari Fasulo

SPRINGFIELD STREET, BIRMINGHAM

The immortal revenge,
Listen, listen, how loud
Is the immortal revenge,
How sweet is the night
In Springfield Street poverty,
The immortal revenge:

The immortal revenge,
Among the torments
Of your lonely heart,
This welcome time of life,
Of love, the immortal revenge:

The immortal revenge,
To hear the bell toll touches
Your soul's heart, very deeply:
Feel the immortal revenge:

Edmund St George Mooney

SILENT ADMIRER

Violet scent and lark song
A cloud like a lost sail
Drifting across the blue
Wheat dancing to wind song
Poppies on spindle-shanks
Flirting frivolous headgear:
I stand waiting, longing for
        a sight of you,
You come and my heart throbs
        thanks,
But deer-shy, I hide until you
        disappear.

Mary Frances Mooney

CRYSTALS OF LIGHT

Crystals of light fall from the sky
Like diamonds from angels glistening as they fly
Cascade like memories as they fall by my side
A reflection of a romanticised image
Wells in my eyes

Echoes of children contented for free
I'm touched by the thought that this used to be me
Walking inch-deep leaving tracks in the snow
But all will be gone when the winter wind blows
Covered with new like all things in life
Crystals fall to the floor, this time from my eyes

For a year-long wait with no promise remaining
The nostalgic thoughts these crystals are containing
Then melted to memory
By the warm morning sun
And banished to the past
Along with the fun

So till next year when angels fly by
And cover my house with white laughter from the sky
And we're surrounded by smiles that haven't cost a thing
These are the memories that I think snow brings.

Paul Jarrett

THE NEW SCOTTISH PARLIAMENT

Scotland is now for Scotland,
Years or turmoil set amidst its beauty,
Y'canna blame anyone else now,
It's up to Scotland now!

Stuart Collinson

JUST FOR THE RECORD

My waking hours are not consumed with schemes
Of grand seductions, intricately planned.
Nor are my nights awash with febrile dreams
Of visceral passion or a one-night stand.

That you should cast aside all other care
And, on the instant of my plea, pay heed,
Forsaking duty, or another's prayer,
Is not my expectation, or my need.

Not looking for lust, with love as disguise,
Not sometimes, or meekly, subject to guile,
I offer friendship and all it implies.
My asking is simple, just make me smile.

It is what it is, what need of a why,
If it's of worth, there it lies in your eye.

Rad Thomas

QUESTIONS

Mother
Don't you love me?
Because you hurt me so bad

Brother
Don't you like me?
Because you know I make you proud.

Chloé AEM Humphries

GOING UP AGAIN

'Just look at him, he's never stirred,
Since the BBC has asked for more,
He's gone and pulled his hair out,
Now his head is feeling sore.
Last year those fools in Labour,
Gave them a five-pound rise,
No wonder most Labour voters,
Say that they despise,
Why must they be so stupid
To give more money to the BBC?
It's plain they don't think of New Labour voters,
And they certainly don't think about me!'
'Calm down, my dear, I don't want you,
To have a heart attack.'
Now New Labour's published their intentions
They can't very well take them back.
Well this will put the people's backs up.
All MPs the public fear.
Just wait until the licence fee
Reaches two hundred pounds a year!

James Ayrey

GUY FAWKES

Bangers, rockets, cartwheels, sparklers
Scaring the living daylights out of people
Dogs barking
What's that?
Sounds like bombs
Scaring the Pakistani shopkeeper
(And his wife).

Sheona Morris Campbell

FORGOTTEN CHILDHOOD

Home from school early
Why is that?

Ran like hell to avoid 'them'
Why is that?

No bruises to show, no wounds to be seen
Why is that?

They taunt, they tease and they touch
Why is that?

I can't be stronger
But I can be faster
So I'll run, and run, and run
That's how I'll beat them.

Joanne Patchett

GUESS WHO AT HALLOWE'EN?

Whisperings, rustlings,
Mutterings in the dark.
Gate creaks. Is it the wind
Or supernatural being?
A sudden flickering of light
Comes and goes, making the shadows dance
Eerily on my ceiling.
Stealthy movement, soft voices, then
Giggling, guess who or what?
Then knocking,
'Trick or treat?'
It's the children!

Margaret B Beguley

PARITY

She watched him dress
Immaculate shirt
Clean-cut suit
Dashing tie

Money left on shelf

She watched him dress
Tatty T-shirt
Worn-out denims
Trainers

Money left on shelf

Rich, poor
Whoever
Whatever

Still enters
The same vagina!

Val Harman

FOR HARRY MEMLOCK

Amber cat
in a tapestry of greens
leaping to catch
dusk fireflies.

Ellen Peckham

ON HEARING THE NIGHTINGALE

Oh! Shy and sweet nightingale, your song
Seems to descend straight from Heaven.
The feel of your melody so plaintive,
As you hide in the depths of the woodland.
Your sorrowful song seems perpetual.
A song exquisite and ever changing.
It pulls at my heartstrings like a cello,
Both mellow and fulfilling.
Yours is a song deserving,
To be considered the very best,
As it spills forth from your little soul,
Like a prayer of thanksgiving,
Welcoming the long days of summer.
A dull bird, who sings in the thickets.
Yet your place forever guaranteed,
In the world's folklore and fairy tales.
Your song so pure in your telling,
You induce in man both joy and tears.
To hear you on a summer evening, haunting.
The warm air, scented with wild honeysuckle.
Sitting content in a moon-bright bower.
Eyes half-closed in pleasure,
Is to know how it feels,
To spend a brief time in Heaven,
Without the need to demand,
The glory of a celestial choir.
Just one voice which is golden.
Bass notes as mellow as a cello,
Welling from the woodland depths,
At peace, as the world about me sleeps.

Julia Pegg

THE VISITOR

A picture-framed window,
The grassiest knoll,
With humps over mounds of green.
Then dips to a shimmering lake
Where we stroll
And wildlife, scurrying, seen.

Then there in her beauty.
Her neck arched with scorn
To slendering orange beak.
She carefully folds her snowy adorn.
Her morning wanderings to seek.

And closer she waddles
Her grey feet are splayed
As she plods the sodden grass.
And as she comes nearer
I gasp in my mind,
As I see her size in the glass.

A black-rimmed eye, jet-like and cold,
Scans the scene before.
Inquisitive to spy the place,
I see the look upon her face.
An open beak tap-tapping at the door.

The nearness to study
Then suddenly, gone.
The face is fierce, the wings spread wide
She turns away to the shimmering lake,
A fluttering of feathers in her wake.
Her swan song adore.
She visits no more.

Beverly Sweetman

I AND YOU

I am me,
Not you.
I cannot think for you,
Only me.
I'm not perfect,
Neither are you.
I've got a mind of my own,
You've got one too.
No one can make me do things I don't want to do,
I don't know about you.
I behave in a responsible way,
I cannot do that for you.
I've got a voice,
So have you.
I'll speak out against the things
I strongly believe are wrong,
I cannot make you do the same.
I believe in equality,
I don't know if you do.
I hate all this segregation,
I cannot say the same for you.
Every day I pray for peace, and unity,
Throughout the world,
Do you?

Pauline E Reynolds

RICHARD KENNETH LLOYD, MY DAD

I suppose I should be glad, Dad,
I had you thirty-one years.
But didn't want to lose you,
I've cried so many tears.
I had to let you go Dad,
But hope you know this true.
That I didn't want to do it Dad,
And I sat beside of you.
I hope some way that helped you,
Cross over to the rest.
Cos I believe you were taken,
Because you were the best.
That you're up in Heaven with family,
And our dogs that crossed over too.
In my heart you'll keep Dad,
Until my dying day.
Till then I send my love Dad,
In my thoughts each day.
I write this to honour you,
I write for all to see.
Then people will know Dad,
Just how much you meant to me.

Love always, your daughter,

Anne-Marie Lloyd-Barrett

THE TANKS ADVANCE

(Written in imitation of Latin metrical verse -
it seemed an appropriate form for the subject (the start of the Iraq war))

Thundering over the desert,
    tanks advance in formation;
guns pointing straight ahead,
    aiming at - whom - in the sand?

Powerful tracks in the hard sand;
    deafening noise of the engines.
Who could defeat such power?
    Where are the answering guns?

Crashes of gunfire erupt then,
    smoke rises straight from the barrels.
Mushrooms of smoke in the distance;
    no one imagines the pain.

Screaming of victims - but nothing
    reaches the armoured division.
Drowned by the noise of the tanks,
    agonies unseen, unheard.

Steel carapace gives protection,
    untouchable tank crews drive onward.
Monsters of death and destruction,
    bringing despair to the foe.

White flags appear in the grey dust;
    drivers of tanks cannot see them.
Guns continue to roar;
    no one is left to reply.

Come to the point of attack, men,
    open the hatch with supreme care;
step out of your carapace gently,
    examine the body parts there.

Kneel down and search for the idents;
    don't think of the mothers and wives now.
Forget the fate of the children;
    bury the enemy dead

Bury them deep in the desert;
    no one must see what you've wrought here.
No purple hearts for these soldiers,
    no matter how hard they fought.

Guns pointing straight at the skyline,
    aiming at - whom - in the sand?
Tanks advance in formation,
    thundering over the land.

David C Taylor

LIFE

Life is like a rosebud,
The thorns are the bad times,
And the petals are the good.
Once you have found its inner beauty,
It will bloom.
That is when you have found true happiness.

We were never promised that life would be easy,
At times there may be more thorns than petals,
But if you can rise to the challenge,
You'll find the beauty that is within.

Life is but a rosebud,
So be gentle with it.
One minute you have it,
The next you don't,
So appreciate its beauty,
Before it is gone.

Claire Begley (16)

F'KING PERFECT

(the folly of being wise)

'F**k it!' Now there's a thing
There's a statement that can solve everything,

It's wonderfully versatile and disgustingly honest
And it can relieve all the shite that life dumps on us,

It doesn't need a spell check or boring education
It's every man's sound bite with a universal communication,

And it can answer the age-old chestnut
'Why are we here? What's life all about?'
That boneheads and boffins are still trying to figure out,

So what's there to learn? And what's there to know?
When - within its own unique definition, 'F**k it' will answer
Because F**k knows.

So when another load of shite is aimed at your door
Just r-e-a-c-h for those two little words and you'll worry no more.

Jessie Morton

EMOTIONAL CAGE

Love is pain that won't let go
Hurt and misery, churning and woe
Grips your soul and rips it out
Twisting your spirit and tearing it out
Wrenching your self from its transpicuous skin
Leaving a wreck torn between patience and sin
Feelings of utter despair and disdain
Someone tear me away from this pain!
If I could I would break away from my skin
Ripping out all the emotion it traps deep within
I cannot stand any more of this pain
But if faced with its absence, what would remain?

Beverley Morton

IN SEARCH OF PEACE

They say a man is defined by his actions
So what does that make me:
A smoker, a joker, an irate bitch?
I don't even know how to sing you my song
All I know is that I feel wrong.

I call upon you to help me heal.
I need you to wash away the pain I feel
And envelop me with your tender caress
So my path can continue with joy and no less.

I search through the dark corridors of my mind
Never wanting to see exactly what I find.
I call your name each day I wake
Peace, come hither . . . before I break.

I sense your presence, I've seen your face.
I desperately need to be soothed by your soft embrace.
Show me the way, give me a sign
So that I can become what is truly mine.

Helena Jaksic

THE HALLOWE'EN WITCH

See the witch, she rides on high
Her silhouette against the moon
In pointed hat, cat sat behind
On her twiggy, twisted, witch's broom.

Once around the world she flies
Her magic powers have no bounds
Waving her wand, she casts her spell
Leaving us mesmerised on the ground!

Sylvia Behan

APPRECIATING MUM

Through all of her bad times,
Never burdened on us,
All of her great teachings,
Always passed on with love,
Emerging from the storms of life,
She was battered but not broken,
A more wonderful woman you'll never meet,
Truer words never been spoken.
A teacher, a guide,
A mother, a nurse,
Her door always open,
As well as her purse,
We wanted for nothing,
Especially not love,
A real live heroine,
Sent from above.
Accept my thanks for the good you've done,
Your admirer, your friend,
Most importantly, *your son!*

Simon McCreedy

HITCHING A HALLOWE'EN RIDE

Still watching, right through from the beginning,
Always the weird ones have their grip.
In ungraspable connectivities, the flow constructs
Focusing the weird, secret, silent currents
Along the guidelines to the home,
Where the cerulean beside the weirdness
Has tetrahedral form again here.

Michael C Soper

THE SOLACE OF DARKNESS

Why on this night do I find peace?
Why on this night do I find I am whole?
Why on this night do I find acceptance?
Why do I find unison? I feel I shall never know . . .
Surely this is no usual thing
To feel so at one with the night . . .
To feel so comforted by the darkness . . .
To find the shadows remove my entire plight . . . ?
I find solace in the night,
In the serenity of the town,
As all those around me slumber,
I walk freely, as I hear no sound . . .
I have never been accepted,
As my mind and thoughts are frequently frowned upon . . .
Yet I enjoy being alone,
As no one shall worry when I am gone . . .
The night air is so fresh,
So free of pollution,
As I walk the empty streets,
Left to ponder in the silence of my notions . . .
To walk without the fear of angry glares,
Without the stress of congestion,
To be at one with the stillness of the night,
To be free of all of life's tension.
At night I have always found unity,
I have always found comfort with night's tranquillity,
And if I am to be labelled anomalous because of my love for darkness,
Then I am delighted to say; I am guilty!
I am a creature of the night . . .
And I enjoy being free . . . !

B L Summerfield

A Dog Can Do Better Than Mugabe

I was so worried when my blind son went on a global tour.
His first call was Tokyo, Japan, in the Far East. I really wondered
how he would negotiate the busy streets of Tokyo that meander
through the world's biggest city. I was happy when he gave me
a call leaving Tokyo Airport after a happy visit.

His second call was Harare, the capital city of Zimbabwe.
I consulted my funeral directors to prepare a coffin for my son
since I expected the worst from the reckless commuter drivers
in the chaotic and dilapidated roads of Harare. To my surprise
my son phoned me aboard a transatlantic flight heading for
New York, after five days in Harare.

Again my heart was beating faster when I thought of the even
busier streets of New York. I gave him a ring after three days and
to my surprise he was at the busy Kings Cross railway station in
London waiting for the Edinburgh-bound train.

He gave me a call when he arrived at his flat, and I asked him
how he managed the busy and dangerous cities of the world.
His reply was so simple, 'My *guide dog* did the trick, Dad!'

My big question to you, Robert Mugabe, is 'If a guide dog can
lead its owner in the busy and dangerous streets of the world, why
didn't you lead Zimbabwe to prosperity with an abundance of
resources at your disposal? You were left with a *vibrant economy* by the
Smith regime. Maybe a guide dog can lead our country to
prosperity. It's high time you leave the *hot seat.* You have dismally
failed to rule our country.'

Thomas Mutangiri

A Devotee To The Feminine Factor

Every time you pass me by in a noisy crowded street
I admire female totality
From your hair to the shoes on your feet
I have contemplated numerous ideas
Some (perhaps) you won't be impressed
By masculine imaginings that require you to be undressed

Your visual display fascinates me. I am mesmerised by beautiful looks
But the sad commercial degradation
Is in the contents of pornographic books.
From mankind's ancient marvels
Nothing equals the aura you possess
Without 'the feminine factor', there is *nothing* at all to address

My ambition is to savour your body
That I long to caress and kiss
And loitering via breasts and nipples
Would be idealistic and wonderful (bliss)
As I discover each inch of you
Bringing pleasure with tongue and lips
Tracing that beautiful landscape
Across, neck, shoulders, back, waist and hips

Age is not important. Nor colour, height or size
Just to share sweet tender intimacy
(Lightly running my hands down your thighs)
As excitement progresses with urgency
Variation on a theme is certain
My bewitching female, please let's make love
But first of all, draw the curtain.

Anthony Lee-Beyer

THE MAN IN THE PARK

You're always close by,
close enough to touch,
I don't need your time,
It's not an obligation,
I don't want you as mine.

What you see standing behind me,
I shudder to think.
The cold, the emotions, the dark.
Running fast, looking over my shoulder,
Imagining there's another man in the park.

He looks like you sometimes,
But only his reflection,
Everyone looks like you these days,
I've planted millions of men in my maze.
They're all just there to look at.
It pleases me but I can't bear to touch.

I hate their smell,
But most of all I hate
The weight, the breathing.
I lose for a while, everything
That is mine.
Then the weight is gone
And my sickness resides.
Please die away from my sight,
The flames of my hatred are
Very hot tonight.

I think you may be different,
Well, I still have hope.
I think it's best to leave it
And never find out.
When I'm aware of your stare
I quickly pout.
Maybe you are the man in the park.
Feeling strong when you dominate me in the dark.

Pulling my hair, burning my arm.
'Oh no, please, not behind the tree!'
'But my dear!
The cricket pavilion is wonderful,
Just come behind there with me.
Don't struggle now please, just lie still.
If you keep quiet you can hear
The footsteps, the knock on wood.'
Then 'Sshh! Wait a couple of seconds.
There! Listen to the cheers,
Aren't they a heavenly sound
To your ears?'

He leaves, I lie,
I can see faces in the sky.
If I stay too long
They'll soon look like you
Or maybe they look for you,
To see how far you have run.

I won't see you again,
Not until I'm dead.
When I see you in Hell,
I'll grab your hair and twist your arms,
And what you did to me,
I'll let the Devil do to you instead.

Margot Macgregor-Bailey

COKE

My name is Coke
That ain't no joke,
Check out any crack head
They're like the walking dead;
Give me one sniff
I'll leave you stiff.
You think you're cool?
I'll leave you drowning in a pool.

My name is Crack
Don't matter if you're white or black
I'll turn you into a thief
Just for you to get a lift.
Come on, give me a sniff
And I'll cause you grief
Cos I can't be stopped
Once you're hooked.

My name is Mr Cocaine
Mess with me, I'll f*** up your brain,
If you meddle with the dope
I'll leave you sick and broke;
I'm gonna drive you down the drain
And leave you insane,
Stop the crap
And say no to crack.

My name is Dope
With me there's no hope
I'm in your neighbourhood
Deadly like a toxic mushroom.
I'll make you high for a minute
You'll lie and kill to get it,
You mess with crack?
There ain't no going back.

Joseph Nthini

EVIL IS ABSOLUTE

Evil is absolute
It is immense
Beyond comprehension
It reaches wide and high
If unchecked it blots out the sky

Evil is absolute
When it enters
Your thoughts and very soul
It chokes and suffocates
Every and any other emotion

Evil is absolute
It drags you down
To your base morals
When reason and kindness
Become the very enemy

Evil is absolute
Draped in black
It steadily approaches
Unseen until it spreads its wings
But you'll hear no birdsong

Evil is absolute
Yet it fears the light
Its spirit can be broken
It is its desire to overwhelm
That creates its Achilles' heel.

Evil is absolute
It knows no
Half measure
It's complete
In its greed.

Richard Gould

THE SPIRIT OF CHRISTMAS LAST

When Christmas comes, it comes so fast
Only seems like . . . not too long, since the last
To some it just comes far too quick
The rushing around shopping, right in the thick

What do I buy, for the people I know?
They don't really need anything, got plenty of dough
Some might say it's not in the spirit
To see it this way, and sometimes dread it

As a man, the prospect of boxers and socks
And for the ladies, some bits for their golden locks
For the kids, everything seen recently on the 'box'
And for the Mrs, some new suzzies and colourful frocks

The whole thing seems crazy, to celebrate the coming
Of a big, fat man down the chimney, carols humming
To eat your mince pies, and drink your eggnog
And he always turns up, come rain or fog

One year he came, I thought he was a robber
Disguised as Santa, wearing his clobber
Then I knew it was him, before towards him I flew
As from his foot, he scraped reindeer poo

Mum noticed the mess as she stroked our dog
She said it was Fido, who couldn't use the bog
But I knew better, as I was there that night
And Fido uses the garden when he needs a shite!

But despite all this, it is a great time of year
And for most it is filled with joy and cheer
The celebration of a fat man, sack emptied once a year
Which is much more than some of them manage around here

But on the bright side, it's not all bad news
As just look at the kids, as their excitement brews
They're far too excited, even to sleep
And stockings on the wall, most of them keep

It's a time they look to, all year round
Not seeing it like us, which I think is sound
As without kids, it would lose its meaning
That's its real purpose, not wallet clearing

Lee Patterson

TWIGLETS

I'd never had one before.
Oh I know what people
say, they say they're good!
Someone said they preferred tea.

No, I'm wrong. That was
about sex. I think.
Anyways, I'm set.
He'll be here any minute.

I'm so nervous, I want
it to be right. So he can
have one too! Or
is it me . . . just me? I think
it is. Oh God, I'll fail . . .

We were in bed looking at
each other, it had begun.
He didn't kiss, I'm glad.
He smelt of Twiglets.

I didn't want to remember
my first orgasm, well, not with
a man who ate Twiglets.
So I faked it.

Lyndsay Cox

THE START BUTTON OF LIFE

Packing my bags tonight, gonna leave this time for good,
this town is too small for me now, there's nothing left,
the people keep changing different faces every day,
the trees change colours and shape, some die and are replaced,
others grow stronger, family and friends are all gone,
there's no more words to write about this town,
the one you can't even find on a map, one school, one shop
and one pub, the roads seem to get smaller, more houses go up
and again more people arrive, the noise level keeps going up,
I can't take it anymore, the door's locked, the windows boarded up,
the chapter coming to a close, bags by my side, taxi pulls up,
that's up, I'm in. I'm really doing this, a new start, a new me,
so I get a new book as the taxi pulls away and I can see the road
ahead is new and exciting, this is me then.

Dylan Angel Halliwell

QUIET ABOUND

No bounding feet when I come in
Just the ticking of the clock
I stand pondering, wondering; expecting you
Remembering; feeling your cold wet nose
Laughing as you jumped up, licking my face
Doing the twist in the air; almost knocking me to the floor
Things are quiet now; no squeaky toys, just hidden reminders
Your treasured chews; precious bones, that old rubber cracker
The one that drove us mad
You're not here hogging the sofa or the chair
Wish I could stroke you once again, play ball across the floor
But yet! I'm sure I can see you
You're like a puppy, in no pain.

Wendy Brittain

THE VISIT TO THE SURGERY

A visit to the surgery on a cold, dark winter's day
Is as good as any theatre, at least that's what I say
You must pretend to be quite poorly, as you stagger through the door
And the lady in Reception barks,
'Have we seen you here before?'
Then she will ask you where you live
And you will give your name
Which is really all routine as she knows it, all the same
When you have finished with her questions, you go and find a place
Then sit back and have a look round and see each familiar face

There is pretty young Miss Jennings - she can't be on the 'pill'
In spite of the big 'bump' she's hiding, I can't say she looks that ill!
Poor Farmer Giles is there, by gawd, he does look black
But that is not surprising, the old beggar's hurt his back
Mrs Collins from the Village Store really looks in pain
She says, 'Oh lor! I do feel bad - it's me rheumatics yet again'
Lady Fawcett from the Big House sits with her nose stuck in the air
She usually goes 'private' so I don't know why she's there
Her spotty-faced son is with her, he keeps pushing his chest out
The villagers are well aware that he has got their housemaid
                                        up the spout!
Mrs Jones from our local has got herself in quite a state
She mutters, 'If the doctor doesn't see me soon, the pub will open late!'
Mrs Bradshaw is not popular, for she has brought along her son
He is such a little b*****d, that to kill him would be fun!
Poor Jamie, the village idiot yells, 'I have got a boil I cannot show
For if I drop my trousers, me mum is sure to know!'

By now I feel I've had enough and say, 'Well, I'll be on my way'
But the dragon in Reception barks, 'What did I hear you say?
Get back to your seat at once and kindly do not waste my time
For if you don't see the doctor, your medicine will be mine'
Well, I know when I am beaten but I have to have a grin
I don't think my visit to the surgery was really such a sin!

Sally-Anne Hardie

PROGRESSION

Russian - Introduction - Egyptian
Discussion - Appreciation - Flirtation
Intoxication - Seduction - Indecision
Inebriation! - Permission
Titillation - Stimulation
Contraception - Penetration
Position Alteration
Repetition - Variation - Repetition
Experimentation - Repetition
Protection malfunction! - Insemination
Deflation - Satisfaction - Valediction

Conception
Desperation - Ruination - Termination?
Desolation - Isolation
Incubation
Production - Creation
Fascination!
Lactation - Perambulation

Calculation
Notification
Recrimination
Accusation - Litigation - Interrogation - Cross-examination
Rejection - Humiliation
Denunciation
Strangulation! Decapitation! Castration!

Recollection! - Communication
Reconciliation
Carnation
Jubilation

Cohabitation
Adoption
Domestication
Multiplication - Repetition
Sterilisation
Superannuation.

Patricia Carlton

BOYS' TOYS

Muffler growls
       Engine roars
            Tyres screech
                 Rubber burns
                       Front lifts
                             Forward lurch
                    Gathers speed
             Driver hunches
        Fist revs
   Speed increases
Vibration excites
        Roundabout ahead
            Lean right
                Knee touches
                      Motorcycle wobbles
                Bike slides
          Rider tumbles
      Silence comes
Ambulance arrives
       Body broken
          Brain dead.

Polly Davies

Love Is...

letting go of a drowning hand
when you suddenly see
you'll both drown in this sea
with no floats, no armbands
and no sight of dry land
if you cling to each other
and neither can swim.

When the panic sets in and
the thrashing begins and
the gasping for air and the
tugging at hair and the dying
cries of 'Why me? It's not fair'
are carried away on
the wings of a bird . . .

So absurd and demeaning
this death without meaning.

Tina Bass

Break Away

Break away from all of you,
your boundless love and trust,
to venture on a pathway,
of greed, lies and lust.
Hopefully, I will forget,
the riches of your ties,
as contentedly, I seep deeper
in my doomed and sad disguise.
Behind a curtain, I will gently weep
praying that you will see,
heroin holds his prisoners
and tightly grasps the key!

Annie Frame

HAYSTACK

Straw-baled bed
warm from summer heat,
the place of passion
and love's entreat.

Lovers have been here before
in that hollowed-out centre
basking in reflected warmth
on loving penetration bent.

No sign of others.
Kick off shoes. Throw
clothing wildly down
into that scratchy hollow.

Oblivious of all nature
except our own heed
to share each other's
exuberant foreplay need.

Calls of bird life
overflowing, mingling
with our ecstatic cries
in orgasmic fulfilling.

Pleasuring lingers still,
no part unexplored.
Caressing, fondling, kissing.
Were human bodies so adored?

Sweet exhaustion,
lazing naked in the sun -
then, hurriedly to dress
as straying ramblers come.

Jo Allen

A CHOSEN CHILD

Will Father Christmas come to me,
Will he answer my prayers?
I sit with my nose pressed up to the glass,
Please will he show he cares.
I watch the children skipping by,
Holding their mom's and dad's hand,
Chatting and laughing, not a care in the world,
So I watch, wait and stand.
Please will someone love me,
And tuck me up at night?
Will they kiss away my fears,
When I wake up in fright?
Will someone help me to forget the past
So I can have a brand new start?
Can they be there in my bad times,
When I've upset the apple cart?
I sent my letter up the chimney,
And I prayed really hard,
Can my life be,
Like you see on a Christmas card.
Jesus had a mommy and daddy,
And Christmas is a time of love,
Oh please, Father Christmas,
I promise I'll be good.
I don't want any presents,
Just a home to call my own,
And all you have to do is,
Please pick up the phone.
The door has suddenly opened,
Two people are standing there,
'Tom; your new mommy and daddy,
You're being released into their care.'

Father Christmas heard me,
And Jesus up above,
I have a new mommy and daddy,
To whom I can give all my love.

S P Cockayne

THE PASSION OF VICTORY

I lay a kiss upon her neck
Devour her sweet incense
As I caress her breast
Our bodies begin to sweat
Our breath hot and heavy
Her legs stroke my own
Her eyes close as she begins to groan
Passion like fire explodes
Two bodies now as one alone
She gasps as I ride her home
Fingers clawing at my back
Our lips they now match
Another gasp now
As she comes
My job I guess is done
For her passion is mine
Her body now won.

Matthew Holloway

THE WORLD GONE MAD

A little girl, snot on her nose
Can't wipe it clean I suppose.
Don't touch the belts on their laps
In case I get accused perhaps.

'But can I hold your hand for a while?'
(They're frightened of some paedophile)
And even though I've been cleared
The parents still can live in fear.

The world has changed, it's now so sad,
Their cynical minds think all is bad,
And all the teachings that I've had
Have now become a pastime fad.

Sports day now a thing of the past,
Blackboards (now white) have disappeared fast
And nursery rhymes not politically polite
Seen as racist, sexist and corrupt, I expect.

A skipping game through fields and trees,
A little boy has grazed his knee.
But I can't touch his wounded scar
In case they think I'll go too far.

Linda Lawrence

DER KRIEG MIT UNDEREN MITTELN

She stayed at home spending his money
so he worked harder, longer hours.
Depressed by his absence she grew fat
he paid for her counsellor, cleaner and couch.

She told him that marriage is cheap prostitution,
so his love for her remained unconsummated.
Angry at his undemonstrative affection,
she called him an impotent hypocrite.

When he tried to kiss or cuddle her,
she swore men were violent rapists.
When he said, 'Sorry,' and walked away,
she followed him chanting, 'You never listen.'

His friend called her a 'lazy slut',
and slapped her face when she complained.
She cleaned house, found a job, lost weight.
She did everything the friend commanded.

She became the model submissive wife,
hoping the friend would carry her away.
But before she could murder her husband,
he had butchered his friend.

J Myhill

LAST GOODBYE

We said goodbye as usual
It was just another day
Little did we know what would
Happen along the way

We had said our last goodbyes
Albeit we didn't know
'I'll see you again tonight dear'
From my memory still won't go

He left here on that morning train
To go to work and back
Just another journey
On that fated railway track

We didn't know it would happen
On that morning train
Darling how I wish
We could meet up again

What do you do when
A loved one fails to return?
How do you deal with lessons
That they still cannot learn?

It's too late as far as we're concerned
We've lost those we held so dear
But we really don't need these events
That have happened year after year.

Lynne Taylor

AWAKE MY LOVE

It is morning, I lie awake
My love sleeps beside me
I need him to my passion slake
It is a day when we are both free.

We have been married just a year
We have our own little flat
We both have to work hard at top gear
To pay the bills arriving on our doormat.

My love works five nights a week
I work in the office during the day
When he comes home he doesn't seek
To make love, he is tired, not at peak.

At weekends and holidays we bond together
I must always be at my best
I want our marriage to last forever and ever
Our love and passion ensure our union is no jest.

I gently nudge my love and remind him I am here
I want to be loved, caressed and wooed
I will tell him he is my most precious dear
That he is not my fancy man or dude.

He awakes, I cannot resist that adoring smile
He kisses me, I am again in Heaven
It is going to be a wonderful day
And it's only just half-past seven!

Terry Godwin

The Redemption Of Man

So corrupt was he in his fall and reason
He had condemned himself unto himself
To a bleak future of ruin.
He did tear himself apart
Put up boundaries upon differences
Of colour, creed, race, intelligence,
But broke them down with change.
But not in some,
Who continue to put him down
And doom himself to himself.
Only when, those with responsibility, everyone,
Look inward, and see faults
Of greed, corruption, and over-indulgence,
Only when these are broken down
And prejudice cast aside
Can they judge
And ultimate justice will be given.
He will be redeemed.
In time,
He will be redeemed.

Stephen Tuffnell

THE KISS

My dear, the very mention of your name
Can strike the spark which lights my longing into flame,
One lingering touch's enough upon my skin
To turn the smouldering heat to fire within.

I touch your lips my pulse is rising higher,
Your tongue meets mine and fills my body with desire,
Stronger than pain, yes stronger still than fear,
The force which pulls me to your arms my dear.

My insides melt into a churning pool of need,
Ne'er to be sated until you plant your seed,
A surge of longing spurred by searching fingertips,
I sense the power as hungry loins press home against my aching hips.

Our arching bodies pulse as one,
The rhythm of a beating drum
Insists that we fulfil its call
Until, full-sated, we will fall
Fast-flowing through the waterfall,
Whilst rainbow promise glints then sighs
Like petals shed when flowers die.

Yvonne Brunton

THE DISEASE

Who asked you in
said you could be in my life?
What did I do to deserve
being cut down with your knife?

I was the happiest I'd ever been
at last my life complete,
why then did you invade?
Why did we ever meet?

Well I've got news for you
you get no life from me,
whatever you throw my way
I will fight you, wait and see.

I've had years of bouncing back
I'll rise after every fall,
go on I dare you, try
for life I will give my all.

Tracy Sampson

LOVE...

Love's a pain
hurts you again and again
but yet you don't get it through your thick head
cos you wanna be cared for, shown love and affection
but hey, I understand, you're only human!

Rahela Begum

OUR LOVE

We laugh and kiss with emotions rising,
touching places dark and secret.
Feelings well and surge surprising,
bursting forth with moisture sweet.

You touch my breast and set in motion,
a desire to course my veins like thunder.
Burning pain in loins is molten,
our emotions rise and burst asunder.

We lie replete, entwine and panting,
in our love secure and warm.
Caressing touches, complete the dancing,
restful slumber heralds in the calm.

Joan Lister

LOVING FEELINGS

Have you lost that loving feeling?
Have you lost that loving feeling from your heart?
Have you lost that loving feeling?
Then I guess it's time for you and I to part
But if I am mistaken
And love for me is still there
Just tell me that you love me
Then my life you can still share
And we'll look forward to the future
A time for us alone
Building on our love for each other
And creating a happy home.

Diana Daley

CONSPIRACY

I read of a conspiracy to conquer the entire world,
It told of wealth and power and fortunes to behold.
A secret society would orchestrate the coup
The few made very rich, but pawns of me and you.

They would infiltrate the government and have a merry spree
Making laws not wanted by folk like you and me.
Interfering with our morals and our education too
Reducing law and order to suit animals in the zoo

They used to say, 'Crime doesn't pay,' but not today,
The criminals run riot and most get their own way.
From multimillion fraudsters, to vandals in the street
It's making life hell for us: for them it's rich and sweet.

Fat-cat bosses lap up the cream, from the corporate bowl,
Not listening to the pleas of workers elbowed on the dole.
They say there are jobs out there, and I guess it's true.
But look in the job centre, the pay is a pittance too.

So clergy admit adultery, some even wear a dress,
Politicians equivocating, being truthful less and less.
Spin doctors selling all their wares exacerbate the pickle.
Try to pin down who's to blame, and they say you're being fickle.

Dave Mack

ACT NOW BEFORE IT'S TOO LATE!

Whatever happened to Borstal? What happened to respect?
No remorse, people's lives left wrecked
Locked away, punished, in a system that worked
Not a slap on the wrist and more talk, talk, talk.

Courts need more powers to deal with the louts
Old people need to be able to get out and about
Police the streets and take away the fear
If it wasn't for the old folk we wouldn't be here!

You'll be punished if you do wrong
No luxury holidays in faraway Honk Kong
No home comforts, just locked in your cell
We ain't really bothered if it's a living hell.

Teach 'em some respect, bring back the cane into schools
If you don't, they'll walk all over you, breaking all the rules
Lock 'em up, let's rid the streets of crime
Remove it all, dirt, scum and grime

Let's get back to how things used to be
Police on the streets for all of us to see
Make the punishments harsh, the streets safe to walk
Let's have some positive action instead of goody goody talk.

Leigh Smart

NUBIAN

Ebony goddess
A graceful vision
In the savannah
Of my frustrated
Life and times
Caught like prey
In the ivory-white
Beam of your smile
I stay captivated
By your Nubian style

Lying beside you
In a lovers' oasis
I caress and taste
Your mocha-tinged
Flanks
Stunned by your
Caramel sweetness

My daydream is
Pricked
By the barista
Proffering an
Iced mocha:
To cool my ardour.

Fearless

SILK SHEETS

Silk sheets,
Heart beats
Fast, fast;
Last, last.

Silk glides,
Skin slides.
Cover, cover,
Lover, lover.

Silk cool,
Whirlpool;
Down, down,
Drown, drown.

Silk gentle,
Elemental.
Caress, caress;
Yes! Yes!

Silk tough,
Enough! Enough!
Slow, slow;
Glow, glow.

Silk warm;
Yawn, yawn.
Sleep, sleep,
Deep, deep.

Janet Bamber

DARKEST DREAMS

From the darkest dreams of midnight, the master in satin awakes.
Parched unto his very soul, how should this thirst be slaked?
This bitter thirst cannot be quashed by water, spirit or wine,
But only the juice of the finest rose, a mistress on whom to dine.
The mistress though is not abed, in nightmares she doth seek,
Preying upon the lonely souls, the lost, the drunk, the weak.
For vampyre is the mistress, a creature of the night,
Her succubitic hunting by the palest of moonlight.
An eager smile across his lips, remembering the day
When Lady J first was met and he set her soul astray.
Alas tonight she hunts alone, whilst he awaits her return.
Now he summons a serving wench, to taste the blood he yearns.
A pale child of tender years, fear within her eyes,
Scarce more than a score in age, a tremble in her thighs.
Imperious he summons her to bed, chains her on her knees,
Boldly lifting up her skirt to take what he should please.
His swollen manhood thrusting, deeply piercing through her meat,
The icy cold of his own flesh enveloped in her heat.
As she peaks to orgasm, his member shudders and spurts,
Sinking his teeth within her neck, she barely feels the hurt.
This exchange of life's fluids, one that gives and one that takes,
As he drains her crimson essence, his thirst at last is slaked.
In the darkest dreams of midnight, the master in satin now lies.
The serving wench lies pale and torn, never again to rise.

Corvus Volatus

SYNDROME

And what did he expect?
To send him to an occasion
Where screams were like music
And corpses of decapitated men lounged around him.
What did he expect?
That the boy would become his obscure fantasies of a robotic man
without reason or feeling?

As if the young boy, even in his youth
And his zealousness
Willing to fight for the nation he loved
Could escape the syndrome of war.

In his youth, where his pride is high
And he is like a fighter
His aching body yearning for the body of a young woman he loves
To make love to.
What is he to do with the abundance of *eroticism* and the *raging*
hormones that he is feeling?

So what did he expect?
That for this young man
The rain of bombs and grenades could easily reconcile
With the breath of his young maiden, caressing his ego
What should he do with this raging sexuality?
Who has he become?

So what did he expect?
That when he comes to put down his weapon, when the war is over
So he can effortlessly put down the memories of limbs lying
hither and thither?
An ordinary day in the life of the *warring* soldier.

KCE

Virtual Reality

I saw you last some twenty years ago,
And though I often wonder where you are,
My heart retreats to where fond memories blow,
And insight summons daydreams from afar.

I never saw you in your glory there,
But now the fancy rolls away the years,
And eager eyes undress you, layer by layer,
Till nakedness reveals your hidden fears.

And I am hedged around with guilt and shame
For bringing down your loveliness to this.
I lust as for a thing without a name,
And claim you with the rapture of a kiss.

I lean upon the ripeness of your breast,
And drink the wine that overflows your lips,
And seize your nakedness at your behest,
And feel the thrill of passion in your hips.

And O' the moisture on your burnished skin,
The sweet seduction of your fragrant breath,
Had almost led the senses into sin,
And tied the love knot with untimely death.

Then I awoke and, drawing from the brink,
Re-clothed your beauty with platonic eyes.
The thought was there, and yet the need to think
Restrained me, and afflicted me with sighs.

S H Smith

UNTITLED

To me, my mum was heaven-sent
She picks up all my clothes
She tidies up my bedroom
And listens to my woes
She takes me out to rugby
To swimming and to tennis
Her dad is Grandad Tommy
Her father-in-law is Dennis
She sees me off at nine o'clock
Just outside my school
And then for six long hours
I learn to play the rule
At six o'clock she picks me up
And then she takes me home
Where there, until it gets quite dark
I wander and I roam
My mother's day is never done
From Saturday round till Friday
Because you see in my bedroom
It's a full-time job to tidy
So when I'm big and I'm grown up
I'll really do my best
If I can do the job as well
It will put me to the test
To me, my mum, who I do love
Is always there for me
She is no miracle worker
She's just my mum, you see.

Thomas M Glynn

SERENITY

Where is my peace, my calm?
My healing agent, my psalm?
Today I'm on a mission of madness.
Life has become my opponent
not enough living in the moment,
I need a retreat for my sadness.

Angels bathe me in serenity
unforgiveness hinders my psyche,
help me to actualise my natural state of mind.
My thoughts can be negative and lazy
erratic and super-hazy,
fearing I shall seek what, I don't want to find.

I think my life should be problem-free
before I can really be happy,
now I know I can see things upside down.
In the midst of great turmoil I can feel serene
must ask more faith to enter my dreams,
life seems too serious to clown around.

I try to fathom my challenges
anger and resentment scavenges,
faith floats away as I sit and struggle.
Now it's gone, it was my key
accuse the divine of abandoning me,
I'm as shallow and as deep,
as a sun-drying puddle.

Yet it works itself out, and I get on
there are no bouncers to the doors of the throng,
I believe if it happens, it's meant to be.
It's of the mundane I tire
beg my consciousness rise higher,
and await my fate with calm certainty.

Sam Lord

SYNESTHESIA

Is that a snow-capped mountain I see resonating gently in the
key of D?
Are those the holographs of sound the dolphins send
when they need to contact their beloved friends?

Ahh . . . the visual sensation from the scent of a rose
causes my ears to start listening to my nose
and the taste of the smell that I see in your aura glows brilliant gold
like the sound of rushing water.

The peach-smelling sight of your purple-sounding cry
feels like the taste of the sun in the twilight sky.
The soft pink aroma that accompanies your kiss
is the sound of the sign that reads *'This way to bliss!'*

We've reached eidetic heaven. The union of the senses
where your taste buds start feeling smells and your ears grow lenses.
Your nose can now recognise the colour of the feeling
of the multicoloured noise that synesthesia is revealing.

I think you saw what I said.
I'm sure those pathways crossed over in your head.
You tasted my words and you felt what you heard.

Didn't we smell the shape of those trees and taste the colour
of the breeze?
When we saw the feeling of the sound of peace,
we knew that from our senses we'd be released.

This collision of sensation,
this liberation from the condemnation
of the imperfection of human perception
is a natural process of correction.
The evolutionary introduction of a new dimension.

Jason James Bearne

PRETTY WITH SCARS

Such a beautiful night,
The girl,
She looks so pretty,
Pretty with scars,
Curled up in the corner crying,
Her head in her hands,
She looks up and stares at me,
Those pale blue eyes see right through me,
She can see my soul,
She can see my pain,
Her lips whisper,
'I know what you feel,
I can save you,
I know what you feel,
I can save you,'
She smiled at me,
And led me to the graveyard,
The moon lit us up,
She looked so pretty,
Pretty with scars,
Her eyes staring right into mine,
She can read my mind,
She can see my thoughts,
Her lips whisper,
'I know what you think,
I can save you,
I know what you need,
I can save you,
I . . . love . . . you,'
Then the kiss,
Captured in a perfect moment,
The glimmer of a knife,
Our wrists were cut so deep,
But her eyes never left mine,
Her lips touched mine again,

Our eyes met as we opened them,
We could feel the love,
We could feel the love,
Our lips parted,
We were in love,
She saved me,
We were dying,
She saved me,
She looked so pretty,
So goddam pretty,
Pretty in blood,
Pretty with scars . . .

Scott Ottaway

GERIATRIC THOUGHTS

Very soon I'll be ninety-five
And wonder why I'm still alive
All my mates are dead and gone
Why am I the only one
With memories of the good old time
Of pretty girls and dry white wine?
I know I'm past my sell-by-date
And soon will wait outside that gate
For someone to decide my fate
Will I play a harp, perched on a cloud
Or stoke that fire in a flame-proof shroud?
Will my resting place be a hole in the ground
Or will I be specks of dust blowing around?
Life is full of uncertainty, so it seems, is death
I'll not know my fate while I still have breath
My thoughts are in a mental jam
But frankly, I don't give a damn!

Norman Neild

GRANDPA

I wrote you a poem, Grandpa,
But I'm not sure that you'll ever get a chance to read it . . .
You left us all behind
But it's not like you meant to
It's not at all your fault . . .

I can feel your presence
Even if you are not there
You smile to make up for words not spoken
Laugh in place of your thoughts not conveyed

Everyone says
That you were once normal
You used to be smart, charming, intellectual,
A respected man
But it was all stolen . . .
By an unfair disease, a wicked, incurable
Illness

It has left you a child, a mere shell of a once
Great man, military hero, grandfather, friend
You forgot all that you once knew
It has left me hoping and praying
That you won't
Forget me.

Leslie Evans

ANGER

Anger is hot red,
Like flames burning you inside,
Anger will destroy,
It lives in the heart of a volcano.

Anger is a feeling,
A feeling that will kill,
It likes to spell out danger,
Like a devil, deep down.

Anger takes over,
So stay away, at all times,
Or it'll destroy you,
Destroy you it will.

Self-failure makes it angry,
This causes it to burn,
Fire flames and flowing lava,
Going out of control.

Soon it will come to an end,
With the anger calming down,
It won't be long now,
Till it's happy again,
But the anger will come back,
With the devil deep down.

Callum Smith

SUMMER CONQUEST

Occluding under the gaze of golden rays
It melts away cold futile efforts
Calming the dirge of Earthly death
Abounding in its benignant spell.

Trumpeting the beauty of wit and soul
It outcasts lethargy from her slumber sleep,
Immersing time in senses enchanted
A gentle relief from burdened restraint.

Blossoming into this beginning
Flowers exfoliate vibrant colours
Releasing energy, dispensing depression
Spreading a velvety sheen of habitation.

Bowing in tribute, birds sing bemused
Leaves flutter adorning sylvan pathways
Water gurgles into streaming rivulets
Falling to the mood of glorious nature.

Rejuvenating in this ritual of homecoming
Responding to the call of its creator
The spirit breaks from faint expression
Gathering your warmth as it percolates.

Samina Amjad

MY LOST YEARS

In the silent of night, a tear falls from my eye
as I remember memories of days gone by.
Memories, that once were so real in my mind
but I surrender to my tears, as I try to find
the moments to my lost years.

Softly, silently, I retrace the steps of yesterday
I retread the path I took along the way.
Remembering my rights and all my wrongs
I surrender to my tears, as I re-sing the songs
of the moments to my lost years.

Silent clouds cast over like shadows in my mind
laying down gently, leaving the past far behind.
Sweetly the past holds so many a dream
I surrender to my tears, as I try to redeem
the moments to my lost years.

The silent of night becomes the silent of morn'
as I remember now, how the memories lay so torn.
Memories once so warm, but now grown so cold
I will surrender to my tears, as I try to hold
the moments to my lost years.

Jeff William Milburn

GRIEF HATH NO RELIGION

A mother weeping on the grave of her son
Tears falling on the cold, grey earth
That empty space deep in her heart
For the child she knew from birth

The pain, the anguish when a loved one dies
As your heart is torn in two
The sense of loss, the emptiness
Encompasses just the few

These feelings are not confined
To one religious belief
Catholic, Protestant, Arab or Jew
They all feel the same sense of grief

How can someone in the name of God
Kill and cause such pain?
They go to church and pray for peace
Then go out and kill again

They rouse the crowd up for the cause
It's all in God's good name
But no matter who they kill or maim
The grief is just the same

Let's see these people as they are
Murdering for self gain
The terrorist counts the profit
The innocents count the pain

Next time you're giving to the cause
Or thinking that you should
It could be your loved one next
Lying in a pool of blood

No matter what name you call your god
No matter your belief
The killing of a loved one brings
The same deep sense of grief.

Bill Dooley

CRADLE

I hold you
as you in turn, hold your rag doll.
Tenderly
as a young mother should.
As long as you're able
dear daughter
long may you Cradle.
I hug you
as you in turn rock and soothe.
Lovingly
as a young mother would.
May your hands be soft and your heart, strong and stable
dear daughter
long may you Cradle.
I watch you
as you sing a lilting lullaby.
Longingly
as a young mother could.
At Fireside or Table
dear daughter
long may you Cradle.

Kevin B Clark

THE BARONIAL HALL

The autocratic aristocrats set the abigales ablush
With amorous applications, alarming them anew.
Minstrels made music, melodies and madrigals,
Both maid and master made to mesmerise.

The agile acrobat astounded all with his ability,
His ambidextrous actions truly did amaze.
Merlin the magician, they marvelled at his miracles,
Magical mysteries, miraculous to behold.

At the tables helping, pot boys and servers,
Bringing wine and mead and victuals to enjoy.
In the rushes 'neath their feet, hounds rummaged eagerly,
Investigating everything, keen for their share.

Hazel Statham

FOLLOW CHRIST'S STAR

As by the grace of God another new year dawns,
let us resolve to keep the Christmas message in our hearts.
May our feelings of congeniality, generosity and
humaneness be the message we impart.

Let Christmas abide in perpetuity,
pray its significance never fades.
God sent His Son into the world,
a sinful world to save.

May we, like the wise men, follow Christ's star,
offering our time, our talents, as gifts to be used
right where we are.
May Christ our Redeemer, our Saviour, our Friend,
walk beside us each day to the new year's end.

Malcolm F Andrews

PIGEON INCOGNITO

I finger the ash from our burnt-out desire
It soils my touch and scalds my heart.
Please rise dear phoenix,
Rekindle our misplaced love.
Let us stare at the stars and map our future.
Let us laugh and joke with an air of invincibility.
Let us touch gently setting my skin alight.

Turn off the fluorescent glare of reality.
Turn away from disapproval and deceit.
Turn around so I can read your eyes
And taste the warmth of your smile.

Never thought you could be so selfish as to fly away.
Or was it my fault for imagining a pigeon could be a phoenix?

Jennifer Hill

NUT AND BOLT

Spiral threads perfectly match.
Stretched, tightened up.
Secure for quite a while, now rusted.

To loosen:
tighten slightly first
or
heat up with an intense flame
or
use some corrosive spray.

Do not use a large spanner,
it will strip the threads away
or they will break.

Kostas Hrisos

CARING

(A groom's dedication to his bride)

I care not though the moon should fail to rise,
And the sun should fail to shine;
I care not for seas too broad to cross
Nor peaks too high to climb.
Such cares as these are of small concern
Compared with my care for you;
For you are my sun, my moon and stars
My life and my love so true.
We have vowed to love till our days shall end
And to care all our whole lives through;
Good times and bad times we've sworn to share
Whatever the world may do.
So then, my love, this journey let us take
And face the world together hand in hand;
Our previous lives of self let us forsake,
Finding love and faith and trust in our promised land.

Norrie Ferguson

REDEMPTION

If below the surface and beyond is
If above and beyond is
If the Earth reacts to the violence of man
If a man reacts to the violence of the Earth
If the Earth has a soul
If a man has one too
If a soul has a beyond
If all these things are
If there is a hope of balance
If we will know.

Rauni Luqman

THE STAGING POST

Strikes me as two - always two opposites.
Sunday comes the family, or you drink in your box;
All lonely. Sometimes so warm, and then icy. Chivalry.
20 American cigarettes sit on the old oak table
Old men gather round to mutter, stutter, and destroy evil.
A fire in the corner crackles old timber in the hearth.
The young. The old. Discreet packets of England combust -
Or is it Britain? Or if you are oh-so-cosmopolitan - the UK.
Stranger's secret kissing in the bar's darkest corner;
Rumbly old and grumbly. Young and high with the
Ecstasy of it all. The Sunday papers. North or South.
Psychedelic, militaristic - always about opposites.
Music's pulsing puddle sends waves around the globe, as
Farmers put gates on hedgeless fields to keep something out.
In church every Sunday she is dressed for something big;
She was once held tight by her father around here in long
Gone days. Now she sits on her interest-free sofa in front of her
Fire - mostly gone - no more money to feed the meter.
The family may be here soon - what will they think?
'Please sir, can you spare me some change for a drink?'

James Midgley

MY BEST FRIEND
(Dedicated to my good friend, Colette Davenport)

I know I'm always far away
But you're my best friend and I'm here to stay.
We're under the same moon and stars,
So if you're feelin' like you're on planet Mars,
And your head's in a bit of a fuzz,
Always remember you can give me a buzz.

Melanie McMahon

I Am The Sea

No man may tame me
For I am of the wild, so free
Free for tidal rebellion
For I am the sea

Blue waters running deep
Or ebbing shallow
Rocky tors above and beneath
Shifting sand at my will

Drawing upon the wind
My waves soaring higher
Swells on the rise, up, up,
Rocking, rolling

Hidden treasures, untold wealth
These secrets I'll not divulge
Dream you can
You'll not collect

Dare you dive my waters
Or swim my salty depths
I can take you anytime my friend
For I am the sea

Jeanette Yates

INFORMATION

We hope you have enjoyed reading this book - and that you will continue to enjoy it in the coming years.

If you like reading and writing poetry drop us a line, or give us a call, and we'll send you a free information pack.

Alternatively if you would like to order further copies of this book or any of our other titles, then please give us a call or log onto our website at www.forwardpress.co.uk

**Poetry Now Information
Remus House
Coltsfoot Drive
Peterborough
PE2 9JX
(01733) 898101**